SO-AWZ-228

WHAT YOU NEED TO KNOW ABOUT

GOD

IN 12 LESSONS

MAX ANDERS

THOMAS NELSON PUBLISHERS
Nashville

Unless otherwise indicated, Scripture quotations are from the *New King James Version of the Bible*, © 1979, 1980, 1982, 1990, Thomas Nelson, Inc., Publishers.

Scripture quotations identified by NASB are from the *New American Standard Bible*, © The Lockman Foundation 1960, 1962, 1963, 1968, 1971, 1973, 1975, 1977, and used by permission.

Library of Congress Cataloging-in-Publication Data

Anders, Max E., 1947–
    God / Max Anders.
    Includes bibliographical references.
    ISBN 0-7852-1344-9
    1. God. I. Title. II. Series.
BT102.A48   1995
231—dc20   95–11751
                                                      CIP

Printed in the United States of America

1 2 3 4 5 6 7 8 — 00 99 98 97

Contents

Introduction to the
What You Need to Know Series

You hold in your hands a tool with enormous potential—the ability to help ground you, and a whole new generation of other Christians, in the basics of the Christian faith.

I believe the times call for just this tool. We face a serious crisis in the church today . . . namely, a generation of Christians who know the truth but who do not live it. An even greater challenge is coming straight at us, however: a coming generation of Christians who may not even know the truth!

Many Christian leaders agree that today's evangelical church urgently needs a tool flexible enough to be used by a wide variety of churches to ground current and future generations of Christians in the basics of Scripture and historic Christianity.

This guide, and the whole series from which it comes—the *What You Need to Know* series, can be used by individuals or groups for just that reason.

Here are five other reasons why we believe you will enjoy using this guide:

1. It is easy to read.

You don't want to wade through complicated technical jargon to try to stumble on the important truths you are looking for. This series puts biblical truth right out in the open. It is written in a warm and friendly style, with even a smattering of humor here and there. See if you don't think it is different from anything you have ever read before.

2. It is easy to teach.

You don't have time to spend ten hours preparing for Sunday school, small group, or discipleship lessons. On the other hand, you don't want watered down material that insults your group's intellect. There is real meat in these pages, but it is presented in a way that is easy to teach. It follows a question-and-answer format that can be used to cover the material, along with discussion questions at the end of each chapter that make it easy to get group interaction going.

3. It is thoroughly biblical.

You believe the Bible, and don't want to use anything that isn't thoroughly biblical. This series has been written and reviewed by a team of people who are well-educated, personally committed Christians who have a high view of Scripture, and great care has been taken to reflect what the Bible teaches. If the Bible is unambiguous on a subject, such as the resurrection of Christ, then that subject is presented unambiguously.

4. It respectfully presents differing evangelical positions.

You don't want anyone forcing conclusions on you that you don't agree with. There are many subjects in the Bible on which there is more than one responsible position. When that is the case, this series presents those positions with respect, accuracy and fairness. In fact, to make sure, a team of evaluators from various evangelical perspectives has reviewed each of the volumes in this series.

5. It lets you follow up with your own convictions and distinctives on a given issue.

You may have convictions on an issue that you want to communicate to the people to whom you are ministering. These books give you that flexibility. After presenting the various responsible positions that may be held on a given subject, you will find it easy then to identify and expand upon your view, or the view of your church.

We send this study guide to you with the prayer that God may use it to help strengthen His church for her work in these days.

How To Teach This Book

The books in this series are written so that they can be used as a thirteen-week curriculum, ideal for Sunday school classes or other small-group meetings. You will notice that there are only twelve chapters—to allow for a session when you may want to do something else. Every quarter seems to call for at least one different type of session, because of holidays, summer vacation, or other special events. If you use all twelve chapters, and still have a session left in the quarter, have a fellowship meeting with refreshments, and use the time to get to know others better. Or use the session to invite newcomers in hopes they will continue with the course.

All ten books in the series together form a "Basic Knowledge Curriculum" for Christians. Certainly Christians would eventually want to know more than is in these books, but they should not know less. Therefore, the series is excellent for seekers, for new Christians, and for Christians who may not have a solid foundation of biblical education. It is also a good series for those whose biblical education has been spotty.

Of course, the books can also be used in small groups and discipleship groups. If you are studying the book by yourself, you can simply read the chapters and go through the material at the end. If you are using the books to teach others, you might find the following guidelines helpful:

Teaching Outline

1. Begin the session with prayer.

2. Consider having a quiz at the beginning of each meeting over the self-test from the chapter to be studied for that day. The quiz can be optional, or the group may want every-

one to commit to it, depending on the setting in which the material is taught. In a small discipleship group or one-on-one, it might be required. In a larger Sunday school class, it might need to be optional.

3. At the beginning of the session, summarize the material. You may want to have class members be prepared to summarize the material. You might want to bring in information that was not covered in the book. There might be some in the class who have not read the material, and this will help catch them up with those who did. Even for those who did read it, a summary will refresh their minds and get everyone into a common mind-set. It may also generate questions and discussion.

4. Discuss the material at the end of the chapters as time permits. Use whatever you think best fits the group.

5. Have a special time for questions and answers, or encourage questions during the course of discussion. If you are asked a question you can't answer (it happens to all of us), just say you don't know, but that you will find out. Then, the following week, you can open the question and answer time, or perhaps the discussion time, with the answer to the question from last week.

6. Close with prayer.

You may have other things you would like to incorporate, and flexibility is the key to success. These suggestions are given only to guide, not to dictate. Prayerfully, choose a plan suited to your circumstances.

I can see how it might be possible for a man to look down upon the earth and be an atheist, but I cannot conceive how he could look up into the heavens and say there is no God.
■ Abraham Lincoln

Why Believe in God?

Imagine I am an archaeologist tramping through the steaming jungle of Central America. I have flown to Guatemala, gathered my supplies, hired my support team, and now I'm forging inland toward a site which I believe will reveal the presence of an undiscovered ancient Mayan civilization.

I am famous for my exploits and have published several textbooks on the modern science of archeology, and these describe the discoveries I have made. I'm a Hoosier, and some people have nicknamed me "Indiana Max"!

We are into our third week, hacking our way through nearly impenetrable vegetation. We're approaching exhaustion. The heat rises to 110 degrees during the day and drops only to 90 degrees during the night. With 100 percent humidity, there is never any relief. The plants either stick you, stab you, or slice you. There are snakes above and lizards below. Then, there are the insects. Mosquitoes swarm you like banshees coming after the soul of a newly departed sinner. Ants gouge your skin and inject their venom. Chiggers and ticks lie in wait to have you for dinner. And the noise . . . the relentless din of countless crawling creatures pierces your mind like a burglar alarm going off in the middle of your head.

I'm wondering how long we can keep going. But the possibility of unveiling a lost ancient population center of great wealth and sophistication drives me on. No price is too great. I must find it!

Three days later, feet burning, eyes stinging, muscles screaming their rebellion, we hack our way through a wall of one-hundred-year-old vines. On the other side, rising like a great green diamond out of the jungle floor, is a huge pyramid covered with centuries of lush, tropical undergrowth. Yes, right where I thought it would be.

I take a compass reading and start hacking my way south. Seven hours later, I discover another pyramid. The afternoon of the next day I reach another one, and the next day I discover the final one. I have discovered a huge ceremonial courtyard, a great, square mile of ancient Mayan life. Connecting the four corners is a raised sidewalk, meeting in the center of the four pyramids at a huge altar made of a single piece of stone. It is the ceremonial center of an ancient civilization, lost centuries ago, lying silent and alone, unseen and unknown by modern man, until now.

Here's the big question. How did I know this ancient civilization was here? Why did I go to such effort? Why did we push ourselves to the breaking point to discover this?

Did I just fly to a random spot on the Central American coast and start hacking my way inland? Not likely. That is a good way to die in the green jaws of the jungle. No, here is how I found this lost city: I was flying over the jungle one day, returning to the neighboring country of Belize. From 25,000 feet, the jungle floor has a very consistent randomness to it. No two square miles are alike, and yet it is all alike. It is different, but always the same.

Suddenly, on the horizon, I saw some hills that looked *very* different. Four of them. There was something about these hills that seemed too predictable. They were square at the base, and nature doesn't produce square hills, let alone four of them. When we were nearly on top of them, I could see that they formed a giant square, with each one being an equal distance from the others.

This was no accident, no random product of nature. This betrayed intelligence, design. Someone had been here. Someone was responsible for these "hills." I took a compass reading and made mental preparations for a return trip. I was sure that intelligent life had produced those four square hills, and I intended to have a closer look. *That's* how I found that ancient civilization.

Why Believe in God?

This imaginary story should set the stage for asking the question, "Why would *anyone* believe in God?" Who is this Being that so many people say they believe in, but none of them has ever seen? Polls differ, but some estimate the number of people in America who believe in God at nearly eighty-five percent. Yet no one reading this book has ever seen, heard, touched, tasted, or smelled God. So why does anyone believe in Him? You say, "Well, the people who wrote the Bible heard or saw God in a vision." So? Some people in mental institutions claim to have seen and heard God. Others claim to *be* God, and we don't believe them. While the personal testimony of biblical eyewitnesses is valid, that claim by itself would not convince us of the existence of God, especially since we cannot interview and cross-examine those who lived during biblical times.

Let me suggest a good beginning point for believing in God. It is the same as the beginning point for believing in an ancient Mayan civilization in the middle of the Central American jungle. When you see something that exists and has design, when there is something that cannot best be explained on the basis of random chance, it is sensible to suspect intelligence behind it.

In this chapter we learn . . .

Four compelling arguments for the existence of God:

1. God explains the existence of the universe.
2. God explains the order and purpose in the universe.
3. God explains the uniqueness of humanity.
4. Biblical evidence demands the existence of God.

So it is in life. The universe exists. Not only does it exist, but it seems to embody design, intelligence, and purpose. If life were random, if the universe expressed only raw chance, there would be little reason to believe in God. But there is more design and more suggested intelligence in the universe than most of us have the intelligence to understand. A thousand years ago, without the aid of science and technology, the intricate designs of molecules, individual cells, DNA, and subatomic particles were unknown. The new information which modern science discovers only adds to the impression that design and intelligence are behind the universe. With the advent of subatomic research, molecular biology, astrophysics, and Hubble-telescope astronomy, many things in the universe astound us. We discover such extraordinary complexity and design that even many scientists are beginning to admit that it can't have happened by chance.

And yet randomness, chaos, and chance seem to exist in such events as natural disasters, storms, fires, and volcanic eruptions. This apparent randomness and chaos in nature has given rise in scientific circles to chaos theory. Unlike the optimism of science and evolutionary theory of the last fifty years, chaos theory views nature as acting randomly, making it possible that things may get better or worse, depending on the random blows of fate. And these random blows of fate, according to many prominent chaos theorists, have brought mostly negative consequences. (Dennis Farney, "Chaos Theory," A1, A8).

The emergence of chaos theory is a virtually inevitable consequence of an atheistic world view. The theories of biological evolution and of social progress grew out of the soil of a culture enriched and stabilized by centuries of Christian influence. Yet from their beginnings, the roots of these theories contained the conviction that change from present to higher forms of biological and human social life could occur without God's continuing involvement. Thus taken together as one grand evolutionary view, these are truly both atheistic and optimistic. But evidence of the last fifty years does not support the theory that everything is getting better. In fact, we are living in a time of increasing pessimism when things seem to be getting worse. Therefore, pressure builds either to abandon the hope of the theory or to return to God. Chaos theorists are abandoning hope in the evolutionary scheme of things. That is a logical decision, but it leaves such thinkers without hope, unless they return to God.

It is much more satisfactory to me to return to the God of creation. Certainly there is apparent randomness and chaos in nature because nature has been forever damaged by sin. That damage does not erase, however, the original fingerprint of God's design. The fact is, in the world, we see both complexity, order, and design on the one hand, and randomness and chaos on the other. It is perfectly consistent with Scripture to say that the complexity, order, and design reflect the handiwork of God's original creation, while the apparent randomness and chaos reflect the fact that God's handiwork has been perverted by sin, which affected not only humankind, but also the natural world.

If that's the case, then one beginning point for believing in God is your own experience of imaginatively "flying" over the landscape of life at 25,000 feet, looking down, seeing what exists, and noticing something that suggests intelligence and design. You ask yourself, *Who or what is responsible for that existence and that design?* This inevitably leads to a discussion about God.

When philosophers talk about God's existence, they generally discuss *naturalistic* arguments. Naturalistic arguments do not take the supernatural, the spiritual, or religion into account. Theologians usually include *biblical* arguments for His existence. Properly understood, these arguments are compelling and reassuring.

How Does God Explain the Existence of the Universe?

Every effect must have an adequate cause, and God is the only cause adequate for the existence of the universe.

The ancient square-based mounds on the jungle floor in Central America had to have an adequate explanation. Nature does not create square-based mounds set in a perfect square, with each mound being an equal distance away from the other mounds. It doesn't happen. The only satisfying explanation is that an intelligent civilization put them there. So, too, with the universe.

And as every effect must have an adequate cause, God, we shall see, is the only cause adequate for the existence of the universe.

Only in the last 100 years or so have modern peoples believed that the universe was not created by supernatural power. With the theory of evolution, intelligent people were able believe an explanation for the universe that didn't require a God. But evolutionists still have to explain where the universe came from, and they have only two choices. One, God created the universe; or, two, the universe came into existence by itself. If you believe the latter, you must also believe that the universe was caused by nothing, or that the stuff that the universe came from has always existed and designed itself by chance. That is difficult for me to swallow.

Let's look at the viewpoint that matter is eternal; it has always been here. After an indeterminable length of time, this matter simmered, cooked, boiled, and finally exploded in one great big bang. Matter began flying out to the far corners of the universe, cooled, and formed suns, stars, planets, and moons.

Every cause has its effect.

On our own planet, things simmered, cooked, boiled, and pretty soon life began, for no reason, in primitive forms. Life eventually evolved into plants, animals, and human beings; all through random chance, evolutionary scientists say. It's all one great big happy accident. But there are several lethal flaws with that explanation.

First, scientific evidence doesn't support it adequately. If you believe the evolutionary big bang theory together with evolution, then, as Francis Schaeffer, an evangelical theologian and scholar of the last generation, used to say, you are locked into the equation: "nothing + the impersonal + time + chance = everything there is." The problem is, science itself doesn't support that conclusion, indeed it *can't* support it until that process can be observed. How can something come from nothing? How can the personal come from the impersonal? How can the intricacy, the design, the order, and the symmetry be a product of chance?

Brain Stretcher

As philosophers and theologians debate the arguments for the existence of God, they break them into two categories with these names:

Naturalistic Arguments
1. Cosmological Argument (cosmos = the universe; logos = study of). The universe exists. God explains the fact that there is "something rather than nothing."
2. Teleological Argument (teleos = purpose; logos = study of). The universe has remarkable order, suggesting intelligence and design behind it. God explains the order and apparent design and purpose in the universe.
3. Anthropological Argument (anthropos = man; logos = study of). Man is unique in all of creation. He longs to know who he is, where he came from, why he is here, where he is going. God explains the uniqueness of humanity in creation.

Biblical Argument
The Bible is true to what is. Explanations of reality in the Bible conform to the conclusions suggested by the naturalistic arguments, and there the naturalistic arguments and the biblical record affirm each other.

Second, it violates science. In his book *The Church at the End of the Twentieth Century*, Schaeffer tells about Murray Eden at MIT. Eden was working with a high-speed computer to answer this question: "Beginning with chaos at any acceptable amount of time up to eight billion years ago, could the present complexity of the universe come about by chance?" The answer was absolutely "No." And few scientists think the earth is older than eight billion years. Four to four-and-a-half billion years is commonly accepted. More recently, the British scientist Sir Fred Hoyle, a mathematician and astronomer, calculated that it would take ten to the forty thousandth power years ($10^{40,000}$) for chance to produce even the simplest cell. That length of time is unimaginable, so much older than the present universe is thought to be, that it discounts any possibility that the big bang and evolution caused our universe.

Of course, the big bang theory, as an astronomical theory, is not inherently tied to the biological theory of evolution. In fact, some Christians believe that the big bang theory accurately describes what happened when God created the universe. Nevertheless, much discussion of the big bang theory is linked to the theory of biological evolution, and vice-versa, as if biological evolution were merely a logical continuation of the big bang.

Recently, a futurist wrote from the perspective of a scientist in 2090:

> It seems amazing now that there was a time when science was supposedly the "enemy" of faith, and religion was deemed hostile to technological investigation. The end of atheism and agnosticism became inevitable as soon as computer calculations made improbable the odds that random natural selection [the process central to the theory of evolution] could be the sole explanation for the ever increasing intricacies found in biology. Equally influential was the discovery of multiple universes, which astronomers found at the macrocosmic level and physicists detected in the microcosmic. Science thus established the current Age of Faith, recreating the Creator. Nowadays, only the fool says in his heart, "There is no God" (Richard Ostling, "Kingdoms to Come," 61).

There is about as good a chance that a monkey sitting at a typewriter hitting the keys at random could accidently produce the complete works of Shakespeare as there is that the universe came to be and thus can be explained by chance.

Do you want me to believe that something came from nothing? Or that matter is eternal and that everything there came about by chance? You may be willing to believe that, but I am not. It is no greater stretch of faith to believe in God than to believe in other "causes" for the universe. Whenever you see something, you are driven backwards to ask, "Who created it?" When you get to original matter, you must ask the same. At that point, if you stop and say, "No one created it. It is eternal. It has always been there."—or if you say that "nothing" was in the beginning and that therefore something came from nothing—that simply isn't satisfying to me. It isn't an adequate explanation of cause and effect. Believe it if you want to. Don't expect me to believe it. *It is no greater act of faith to believe in God than to believe what you must if you do not believe in God.*

If I say, "God created the matter," my inquisitive friends will usually say, "Aha! But who created God?" As though they had me.

Not so. There has to be a starting point. You must start with something, or else something has come from nothing, which is nonsense. The question is, do you want to stop with a big ball of mud bubbling in the center of the universe and say that everything there is a result of an explosion in that big ball? Do you want to stop the whole discussion by saying, "The big ball just always was." Or, do you want to stop with an eternal Being who has always existed and will always exist, who is powerful and intelligent beyond our capacity to comprehend? You must stop with a great ball of mud, or you must stop with God. Which will it be? Stopping with God takes no more faith and answers more questions.

But if you choose to stop with the great mud ball, ask yourself honestly, "Why?" Does the objective evidence demand you to affirm the great mud ball; or might your decision to explain everything by "nothing + the impersonal + time + chance" be influenced by your preference for the *consequences* of that explanation, if it be true? For if God exists, that God is the source of all that exists, and you are merely one of many of His creatures. Therefore, you owe your entire existence to His will and are rightly accountable to Him. Clearly the great mud ball, being impersonal, cannot call you to account for yourself. This is why, for many people, the great mud ball is a more desirable explanation—not a truer or better explanation, but a more desirable one.

Listening to Dr. D. James Kennedy, pastor of Coral Ridge Presbyterian Church, on one of his weekly broadcasts, I heard him tell the story of Julian Huxley, a renowned secular humanist. Huxley had been asked why scientists had been so eager to jump on the evolution bandwagon, even though it was an unproven theory. According to Kennedy, Huxley said he thought it was because God was too confining to their preferred sexual mores [customs or standards]! How refreshing to find a man who will admit that he does not *want* to believe in God, rather than saying evidence *prevents* his believing. As we will see, the God of the Bible not only explains the existence of the universe, but it also explains the response of many who, like Huxley, choose not to believe in Him.

How Does God Explain the Order and Purpose in the Universe?

The order and purpose in the universe suggest an intelligent creator behind it.

Not only is the universe "here," and therefore to be accounted for, but its order, design, and purpose must also be accounted for. It is the difference between all the parts of a watch lying in a jumbled heap on a table and having it up and running on your wrist. It is one thing to explain where the jumble of parts came from. It is quite another thing to explain how they all got put together in such a way as to tell time. Not only is the universe "here" but it also runs like a precision watch. If you are going to believe that a Mayan civilization exists on the jungle floor because you see four suspicious hills from 25,000 feet above, how much more should you be convinced of God because of the design and apparent purpose.

The genetic code in a simple DNA molecule is so complex that we have not yet figured out what it is. The atom is made up of protons, neutrons, electrons (and many other subatomic particles discovered in the last fifty years). There is a trillion times more space than matter in the atom. So in my hand, there is a trillion times more space than matter. And there is a trillion times more space than matter in this book. Why doesn't my hand pass through the book?

If that isn't enough, what we used to call matter is beginning to look more and more as if it is not merely matter but little compressed balls of energy. If this is true, then the universe is held together by an amazing power indeed!

Or, how about this one. If you slowed the rotation of the earth even a small amount, you would turn it into a desert on one side, and a frozen wasteland on the other. So if square hills in a jungle *suggest* a Mayan civilization, the universe *shouts* of God. Many evolutionists want to believe in the big bang and evolution, not because the evidence is overwhelming, but because, in their minds, *beginning* with an bias against God, there is no other acceptable alternative.

Order testifies to intelligence.

Sir Fred Hoyle, a highly regarded British scientist, wrote in an article entitled "The Big Bang in Astronomy":

> The latest data differ by so much from what theories would suggest as to kill the big bang cosmologies, but now because the scientific world is enamored by the big bang theory, the facts are ignored (*The New Scientist*, 521).

Robert Jastro, the well-known geologist, physicist, and agnostic, wrote:

> Perhaps the appearance of life on earth is a miracle. Scientists are reluctant to accept that view, but their choices are limited. Either life was created on earth by a being outside the grasp of scientific understanding, or it evolved on our planet spontaneously through chemical reactions in non-living matter lying on the surface of the planet. The first theory places the question of the origin of life beyond the reach of scientific inquiry. It is a statement of faith in the power of a supreme being not subject to the laws of science. The second theory is also an act of faith. The act of faith consists in assuming that the scientific view of origins is correct without having any evidence to support that belief ("God's Creation," 68).

In "The Tailor-made Universe," scientist P. C. W. Davies asks, "Why does it fit so well? It looks like someone made the universe. I don't believe it was made, but it sure looks that way."

No, the scientists do not reject creation because the evidence demands it, but because their approach to science will not allow them to allow God's existence as the beginning point for understanding the universe and life. Thus God or the big bang and evolution appear to be their only alternatives. Were they to approach the data with a will open to the existence and consequences of God's reality, many more of them would find that God alone satisfactorily explains what we observe in the universe.

How Does God Explain the Uniqueness of Humanity?

Humankind is a higher being than all other animals, and being created in the image of God explains why.

Humans are different from animals, and ancient cave drawings suggest that people have always considered themselves different. Man longs to know who he is, where he came from, where he is going. He longs for purpose and meaning. This difference is explained because man is made in the image of God.

Dogs and cats and monkeys have no longing for purpose. They have no longing for immortality. They have no thirst for a creator. Man has a conscience, a moral sense of right and wrong, superior intelligence, and sense of a spiritual domain. He believes that some things are right and wrong. He feels guilty when he does what he thinks is wrong. These are not mere evolutionary developments. They are special capacities given to man by God, who has not given them to animals. Pigs don't commit suicide out of despair over the meaninglessness of life. Kangaroos don't revolt against their superiors because of discrimination in the herd. Penguins don't form support groups to help each other deal with personal trauma. Wildebeests don't record their history or trace their family trees. Buffalo never draw crude sketches of themselves on a cave wall.

Humans are different from non-humans. They are higher than the animals. They are superior, not just in the quality and quantity of their intelligence, but also in their spiritual nature. One century of **Humanity differs from the animals.** atheism is about all the atheism you can find in history, and it is on its way out as a dominating cultural force. The American Atheist Movement, led by Madalyn Murray O'Hare, is losing members rapidly and, by her own admission, is on its last gasp.

The Soviet Union disintegrated and the church in the former Soviet republics grew. The church in China at the time of this writing is repressed but growing rapidly. In the United States, there is a dramatic revival of religion, though much of it is not Christian. The time may come when, as a society, we may look back on atheism and say, "How profoundly short-sighted and narrow-minded!"

God made us superior to the animals and intended us to live accordingly. The more humanity forgets God, the more like mere animals people will act. But unlike animals, people have the capacity to change.

How Does Biblical Evidence Demand the Existence of God?

The Bible concurs with our observations about life and the universe, and describes the God who made it.

We have not begun by looking at the Bible to answer our wondering about the existence of God. If we had, you might have objected that appealing first to the Bible is like asking someone on trial to be his own character witness. On the other hand, you would expect the Bible to concur with reality.

The Bible affirms our looking at the universe for initial evidence for the existence of God:

The heavens declare the glory of God; and the firmament shows His handiwork (Psalm 19:1).

O LORD, our Lord, how excellent is Your name in all the earth, who have set Your glory above the heavens! When I consider Your heavens, the work of Your fingers, the moon and the stars, which You have ordained, what is man that You are mindful of him, and the son of man that You visit him? O LORD, our Lord, how excellent is Your name in all the earth! (Psalm 8:1, 3, 4, 9).

God intended the intricacy and design of the universe to point to Him. Concerning that intention, Romans 1:18–20 reads,

For the wrath of God is revealed from heaven against all ungodliness and unrighteousness of men, who suppress the truth in unrighteousness, because what may be known of God is manifest in them, for God has shown it to them. For since the creation of the world His invisible attributes are clearly seen, being understood by the things that are made, even His eternal power and Godhead, so that they are without excuse.

Concerning the uniqueness of humanity, the Bible says in Genesis 1:26 and 27 that God made man in His image and likeness, male and female.

Who has not sat on a moonless night, when the stars seemed so bright they might fall from the sky, and had the thought well up, "There must be a God"? Who has not looked at the beauty of

the Grand Canyon, or Yosemite Valley, or the
Pacific Ocean, and thought, "There must be a
God"?

The Bible proclaims that the universe reveals God.

Such human experiences of the glory of cre-
ation often prompt just the response that the Bible everywhere
presupposes and exclaims, "There must be a God!" The Bible's
consistent witness that God exists and the naturalistic arguments
we have considered together amply justify believing in God.

How May a Skeptic Seek Out God?

If you have for some reason already decided that you do not
want to believe in God, then you can devise evidence to support
your decision. Deciding that you won't believe in God is like deciding ahead of time that you don't have cancer, and therefore,
you explain away all the evidence that might suggest that you do.
Yet what you *think* about whether or not you have cancer is irrelevant. What is relevant is whether or not you *have* it. Therefore,
the only safe course of action is to look at all the evidence and be
willing to modify your initial decision when you find the evidence compelling.

If all this were merely a matter of intellectual curiosity, we
could debate it until we ran out of energy, ended in a stalemate,
shrugged our shoulders and said, "Well, that was interesting, but
I guess there's no way to know for sure." Then we could go home
and think about something else.

But it is certainly more than an intellectual debate to me. I
want to know there is a God. I want to know if it is safe to die, I
want to know if there is something I can do to make everything
okay for me when they lay me six feet under and throw a shovel
full of dirt in my face.

In addition, I also want to know if it is safe to live. I want to
know if there is purpose and meaning in life now. I want to know
if I am going through life on my own, at the mercy of random
blows of fate, or if there is a God who loves me and will guide me
and look out for me. I want to know if there is someone I can pray
to, or if I am alone. I want to know if there is such a thing as truth
and error, right and wrong. When I lose my job, when my family
falls apart, when my health fails, when the wrong person is
elected, when my home is devastated by a tornado, or my town
is ravaged by a flood, is there a God? Will He see me through the
trials of life? Is it safe to live?

I'm not content to dismiss all this as an interesting intellectual debate. I'm not content to leave this as a stalemate. I want to press through the stalemate. If we cannot scientifically prove or dis-

---

Why I need to know arguments for the existence of God

1. To avoid falling into ancient false belief systems already identified and discredited in church history.
2. To avoid being deceived by a present-day cult or false religion.
3. To strengthen my own faith and walk with God.
4. To be able to speak intelligently about God with others.

---

prove God, I want to know the likelihood of His existence, and then go with that likelihood and seek knowledge of Him in an appropriate way.

I'm not going to jeopardize my eternal destiny or present sense of meaning and purpose in life by deciding ahead of time that there is no God, and then interpret all the evidence in light of that presupposition, without searching for God in ways appropriate to such a search.

The last part of the previous sentence is important because many people who do not believe in God claim that they have, in fact, considered all the evidence before stopping with their unbelief. But "all the evidence" includes not only the naturalistic arguments and the biblical testimony, but also a willingness to approach God (should He exist) in ways appropriate to finding Him. The principle here is common to all human searches for knowledge: The method of inquiry must be appropriate to the object of knowledge. You don't, for example, learn about nuclear physics by interviewing drinking buddies. And you don't learn how to love your wife by analyzing the molecular structure of her perfume. Neither do you learn how to sky dive by flying paper airplanes. That which you want to learn must be pursued in an appropriate way. If you want to learn of or know God, you must search for Him in a way that leads to Him.

God is found through an appropriate search.

What does this principle mean, applied to knowing God? While we discuss knowing God more fully in a later chapter, here we can identify a few crucial characteristics of any good-faith effort to know God and thus to fully consider "all the evidence."

Based only on what we have discussed in this chapter, what is God like? The God who created the universe with innumerable structures and processes that occur daily and with the breathtaking diversity of plant and animal life we can observe—this God is, at the least, the supremely intelligent, creative, and powerful Being of the universe. And the Bible consistently witnesses to the personal quality of this Being: He communicates with His creation and desires an ongoing, authentic relationship with humanity.

So, apart from any scientific or philosophical methods and techniques we might employ to know of God's existence (such as the naturalistic arguments), how do these characteristics of God help us know how we should approach Him: If God is, He is a Being whom we should approach only with the highest respect and in the most profound humility. He would not be just another cell to be scrutinized under our microscope, or a galaxy to be measured by our radio telescope, or even a peer we may approach casually. He would not be an object to be mastered, but a Master to be honored and obeyed. And only when people approach Him in humility, seeking to know Him on *His* terms, in His way, can they claim to have examined all the evidence concerning His existence.

If you do not know God or haven't yet made up your mind about His existence, don't stop your inquiry before bending your knee in honor to Him and in humility before Him, asking Him to make Himself known to you. If the prospect of approaching God in this way repulses you, at least you know that there's more to *this* inquiry than a cool, detached, impersonal sifting of evidence: You have bumped into the main reason people don't believe in God—their wills.

Julian Huxley confessed that his scientist colleagues embraced evolutionary theory so quickly because it did not challenge their morality, while the God of the Bible certainly did. If we see that the naturalistic and biblical evidence makes the existence of God plausible, but we still resist acknowledging or bowing before Him, we should face the true source of our resistance—not external facts (or a lack of facts), but our internal will. We are unwilling to give ourselves over to Him, which is what He requires of those who would know Him. Repentance and obedience are the key elements in a search for God, and these actions strike the deathblow to our autonomy and freedom from ultimate accountability. So naturally we resist bending the knee. But that is finally the only way we can really both know that God exists and know him.

And, ironically, when we do find God we discover that it was He who found us. Apart from God's grace, we don't want to know Him. He places in our hearts the desire to know Him. He leads us in our search. When we come to love God, we discover that it was He who first loved us.

Conclusion

Do you want to know God? That is exciting. It indicates that God Himself, the Creator of the universe, is knocking on the door of *your* life. In a spirit of repentance and obedience, let Him in. Tell Him that you believe in Him fully. Tell Him that you are willing to repent of your sins and that you want Him to come into your life and help you to become the kind of person He wants you to be.

When I first came to know God, it was in a time of personal confusion and turmoil. I said, "God, if you are there, do something. Let me know." He did something. He let me know. He led a person into my life who explained how I could know Him. He will do the same for you, one way or another. God will not turn away anyone who turns to Him, and He has promised that any who seek Him honestly and diligently will find Him (see Jeremiah 29:13).

In summary, whatever you think about ultimate matters—how the universe and life came to be, or whether or not God exists—you believe by faith and not simply by unambiguous, overwhelming, public evidence. Even if you do not believe in God, you are still exercising faith. So why believe in God? Because He fully explains the existence of the universe, its complexity, purpose and design, and the uniqueness of humanity. Only God explains these and also offers Himself to be known by those who diligently seek Him.

Speed Bump!
Slow down to be sure you've gotten the main points of this chapter.

Question
Answer

Q1. How does God explain the existence of the universe?

A1. Every effect must have an adequate cause, and God is the only *cause* adequate for the existence of the universe.

Q2. How does God explain the order and purpose in the universe?

A2. The order and purpose in the universe suggest an *intelligent* creator behind it.

Q3. How does God explain the uniqueness of humanity?

A3. Humankind is a higher being than all other animals, and being created in the *image* of God explains why.

Q4. How does biblical evidence demand the existence of God?

A4. The Bible concurs with our *observations* about life and the universe, and describes the God who made it.

Fill In the Blank

Question
Answer

Q1. How does God explain the existence of the universe?

A1. Every effect must have an adequate cause, and God is the only _____ adequate for the existence of the universe.

Q2. How does God explain the order and purpose in the universe?

A2. The order and purpose in the universe suggest an _____ creator behind it.

Q3. How does God explain the uniqueness of humanity?

A3. Humankind is a higher being than all other animals, and being created in the _____ of God explains why.

Q4. How does biblical evidence demand the existence of God?

A4. The Bible concurs with our _____ about life and the universe, and describes the God who made it.

For Discussion and Thought

1. Did you believe in God before you read this chapter? If you did, why?
    Does this chapter add to the reasons why you believe? How does it
    confirm your belief?

2. If you did not believe in God before reading this chapter, how has this
    information affected your perspective?

3. Name a reason to believe God exists other than those discussed in this
    chapter.

4. If a child wanted to know about God, what would you tell him?

5. How does your family history or personal experience influence your
    belief in God and what He is like? How does it influence your ability to
    trust God?

What If I Don't Believe?

Ancient False Theories
In Western civilization there are three common historical alternatives to
believing in the existence of God.

1. Agnosticism: the belief that you cannot know God even if He does exist.

2. Atheism: the belief that God does not exist.

3. Pantheism: the belief that all forces and objects in the universe are God.
    Rocks, trees, animals, the earth, and humankind—all are part of God.

Present-Day False Theories
Added to that list are two modern alternatives to disbelieving God's existence.

1. The New Age Movement. This movement has been characterized by a
    general reliance on pantheism, paganism, reincarnation, and the revival
    of the supernatural.

2. Secular Theology. Though this term is inherently contradictory,
    nevertheless, there are those who work within churches and/or

denominations who, in spite of that incongruity, do not believe in God as the Bible describes Him.

Personal Results

There are several common personal consequences of not believing in the existence of God.

1. You are forced to explain the existence and design of the universe with the equation: nothing + the impersonal + time + chance = everything there is.

2. You have no answers to the classic questions of meaning for humans: Who am I? Where did I come from? Why am I here? Where am I going?

3. The past is viewed as a meaningless accident then death is viewed as meaningless annihilation. If you are sandwiched between a meaningless past and meaningless future, you cannot escape a meaningless present.

Societal Results

1. There is no basis for absolute truth. Since there is no God, there is no communication from God to explain what is right and wrong. The Bible, then, is just another book. Therefore each person is left to himself to decide what is true, truth becomes perceived as relative, and there is a breakdown of agreement in society as to what is right and wrong.

2. Since each person is morally free to determine for himself what is right and wrong, many people decide to disregard written laws. Crime and social disintegration accelerates.

3. Human life then becomes diminished since it is no longer seen as created in the image of God. Man viewed as an animal or bio-mechanical machine begins to treat himself accordingly. Abortion, euthanasia, genetic experimentation, and so on become accepted norms.

For Further Study

1. Scripture Passages.

At least seven passages in the Bible speak of reasons to believe in God. They are:

- Job 38:1–39:30
- Psalm 19:1–6
- Ecclesiastes 3:11

- Isaiah 40:12–17

- Isaiah 40:26

- Acts 14:17

- Romans 1:18–20

Read these passages and consider how they integrate with arguments for God's existence.

2. Books.

There are seven helpful books for studying this subject further. They are listed below in general order of difficulty. If I could only read one of these, I would read the first one:

Know Why You Believe, Paul Little
Know What You Believe, Paul Little
Basic Christianity, John Stott
Mere Christianity, C. S. Lewis
The Church at the End of the Twentieth Century, Francis Schaeffer
The God Who Is There, Francis Schaeffer
He Is There and He Is Not Silent, Francis Schaeffer

2

Who Is God?

Marilyn vos Savant, a brilliant lady who reportedly has the highest I.Q. ever recorded, writes a syndicated column in which she answers tricky questions from people who want the benefit of her intelligence. Someone wrote to ask her what was the most powerful idea that she knew of. She replied that "truth" was the most powerful idea she knew of, because it is not affected by how we relate to it. Whether or not we know it, or whether or not we agree with it, doesn't matter, because truth is still true.

That seems like such an undisputable answer, and yet many people would not agree with it. Today, the dominant opinion in American culture is that truth is relative. What is true for you might not be true for me. Or what is true today might not be true tomorrow. And certainly, there are limited times when that perspective is correct. For example, one child's mother might not allow him to cross the street. Another child's mother may allow her child. So whether a child should cross the street appears to be relative—right for one child and wrong for another.

But we are not talking about such obvious matters. We are talking about whether absolute truth even exists; that is, truth which is true for all people everywhere whether or not they know or agree with it. Some believe that no absolute truth exists. Period. Even physicists, people whom you would think would be forced to believe that absolute truth exists in the laws of physics, are beginning to waffle on the matter. Even the laws of physics, say some physicists, are relative (although I see no physicists trying to fly off the Empire State Building, because gravity seems pretty consistent!).

As a result, talking about God is becoming difficult even among friends, because people are having trouble agreeing on what is true. When you ask a group of people, "Who is God?" you may get any number of conflicting answers. Fifty years ago in the United States, you would have gotten a pretty uniform answer. Today, you don't. Just as truth is relative in the eyes of most people, so their concept of God is relative. Each person feels free to decide for himself who God is.

Many people agree that "God is a very personal thing—which does not mean that He is a person. It means that each person has the opportunity to devise his own notion of what is God to him. That's sacred. None of us has the right to take that away from anyone else—which is to say that if we do, we are transgressing on something pretty heavy"(*What Do We Mean When We Say God?* Deidre Sullivan, 95). A little hard to follow, isn't it? That's the way conversations get when you abandon absolute truth.

In this chapter we learn . . .

1. A definition for what we mean when we say "God."
2. What characteristics God has that humans also share.

If there is a God, then no matter what we mean when we say "God," it has no real value unless *God* says the same thing. If there is a God, He is who He is, regardless of what we think. Our attempt to "wish" God into being what we want Him to be is nonsense. A book entitled *What Do We Mean When We Say God?* compiles the answers of thousands of people who were asked that question. Some of the answers in it sound profound, but many are in fact inane. One person wrote, "My opinion of God is that everyone sees God in their own way. I see God as being black because I am black. In the same breath, a white person might see God as being white. I have no objection because we both have the same God, we just see Him differently." Another wrote, "The feeling I get from the word 'God' is one of love. I think He is a very different kind of being, a kind, gentle thing—in a way, Santa Claus comes to mind. I know Santa Claus is not real, but if he was, God would have the exact personality of him"(117).

I marvel at the short-circuited thinking that can invent and believe a definition about God without any verification. I don't think people understand how foreign this kind of thinking is to religious belief. There is not one major religion in the world that gives anyone the freedom to invent his own definition of God. Islam doesn't. Judaism doesn't. Christianity doesn't. Even Hinduism and Buddhism set limits to their meanings of God or god(s), as does so-called New Age thinking. Nevertheless, because truth is absolutely relative today, many people ignore what religions teach about God. As a result, they make up their own definitions, and then talking about God ends up in a ball of confusion.

How Do We Define God?

God is an infinite, eternal spirit, creator of the universe and sovereign over it.

While this definition is not complete, it is accurate as far as it goes. It would take a large book to define God fully, and even then it would be incomplete. But here we have a starting point. When we refer to the God of Christianity, our definition of God is not left up to our own discretion but must be determined from the pages of the Bible. Individual speculation has no more validation than a roll of the dice. The God we are talking about is the creator of the universe, the original being, the sovereign ruler of all that is, the sole judge of all that is true and false, right and wrong, good and bad. He is the One who communicated to humankind generally in nature and specifically through the words of the Bible.

The fourth question in the Westminster Shorter Catechism, a teaching curriculum used in many Presbyterian churches, is "What is God?" The answer is, "God is a Spirit, infinite, eternal, and unchangeable in His being, wisdom, power, holiness, justice, goodness and truth." This is a statement which the late theologian Charles Hodges described as "probably the best definition of God ever penned by man."

> **God is infinite and sovereign over creation.**

We must know God if we are to trust Him. We must trust Him if we are to obey Him. We must obey Him if we are to have meaningful life on earth and eternal life in heaven. And we can only obey Him if we know who He is; that is, what His characteristics are, what He is like.

Why I Need to Know Who God Is

Today, there is no common understanding of who God is. Many people make up their own definition of who God is. We must be sure we are talking about the same God when we address the question, "Who is God?"

When discussing what God is like, it is helpful to divide His characteristics into two categories: those He shares with humanity (sometimes called his *moral attributes*, or his *communicable attributes*), and those He does not share with humanity (sometimes called his *natural attributes*, or his *incommunicable attributes*, which are unique to Him alone).

The characteristics that God shares with humanity are greatly diminished in people, but they are similar enough to allow a relationship to exist. An analogy may be seen in the relationship between people and pets. While a person's intelligence and emotional makeup are far superior to a dog's, the dog has enough intelligence and emotional capacity for both the owner and the dog to have an enjoyable and satisfying relationship.

My wife and I used to have a large black standard poodle. The image that pops into your mind when I say that would be quickly dispelled if you were to have seen her. For example, we did not give her a "poodle cut." We cut her *au naturel*. Every hair on her body was about two inches long. She looked much like a black sheepdog. In many ways she was intelligent, but in some ways she seemed retarded. She never obeyed us, but she almost always agreed with us, so that we lived together rather harmoniously. She was so smart that there were certain words my wife and I could not say in conversation with one another, words like "ride," "food," "treat," "car," "vet," and others. If we said them, she flew into a whirling dervish of anticipation. If we spelled them, she became inquisitive. She was the most sanguine dog I have ever seen. Everywhere we went, she thought she was leading a parade. She would grab a stick or something, throw her head in the air and bounce along in front of us as though she had been given the key to the city. Our neighbors loved her, our friends loved her, and even our vet loved her. Everyone loved Sugar Bear. She had enough intelligence and emotional capacity to endear herself to us. It was a dark day indeed when she was killed by a large truck (she hated trucks). She was either too dumb or too smart to be broken of the dangerous habit of chasing trucks, and in the end it proved fatal.

I don't want to insult anyone by comparing him to a dog. I just want to make the point that living things do not have to be on an equal plane in order to have a meaningful relationship. We loved Sugar Bear, just as many of you love your pets, even though they are not on an equal plane with you.

Therein lies an analogy between mankind and God. We are not on an equal plane with God, but we share enough characteristics with Him that we can have a meaningful relationship with Him. Therefore, when addressing the question, "Who is God?", it is helpful to look at characteristics that God and humanity have in common which enable humanity and God to have a relationship.

What Characteristics Does God Share with Humanity?

Among the characteristics which God shares with humanity are His holiness, love, justice, and goodness.

Holiness

The holiness of God is difficult to define. Most definitions are so technical that an average person gets lost in the words and cannot grasp or appreciate what is being said. I am going to try to simplify the concept, which requires caution because you run the risk of distorting the truth. To prevent that, though, I will not say everything that could be said about holiness. I will try not to say anything inaccurate. When a basic grasp is gained, more complex and complete explanations may be studied later.

In completely reduced form, holiness means "without sin." To say that God is holy is to say that He is without sin. Yet we must say more. Not only has God never sinned, He is incapable of sin. That is His character, His very nature. Anything that is like God is not sin. Anything that is not like God is sin. It is not that He conforms to some high standard. He *is* the standard. Holiness means, on one hand, a complete absence of moral evil, but on the other hand it implies moral perfection. All that is good is bound up in God's character. Anything that departs from God's character is evil.

Holiness is God's most clearly defining characteristic. We see two dramatic statements concerning the holiness of God in Scripture. One is in the book of the prophet Isaiah:

In the year of King Uzziah's death, I saw the Lord sitting on a throne, lofty and exalted, with the train of his robe filling the temple. Seraphim stood above Him, each having six wings; with two he covered his face, and with two he covered his feet, and with two he flew. And one called out to another and said, "Holy, Holy,

Holy is the Lord of hosts, the whole earth is full of His glory." And the foundations of the thresholds trembled at the voice of him who called out, while the temple was filling with smoke.

Then I said, "Woe is me, for I am ruined!

Because I am a man of unclean lips,

And I live among a people of unclean lips;

For my eyes have seen the King, the Lord of hosts."

Then one of the seraphim flew to me, with a burning coal in his hand which he had taken from the altar with tongs. And he touched my mouth with it and said, "Behold, this has touched your lips; and your iniquity is taken away and your sin is forgiven. Then I heard the voice of the Lord, saying, " Whom shall I send, and who will go for Us?" Then I said, "Here am I, send me."(Isaiah 6:1–8, NASB)

From this passage, we learn why holiness is God's most defining characteristic. This is a vision of the Lord in the temple.

God is holy. God is high and lifted up. Smoke is filling the temple. The whole temple, which was a solid, sturdy building, shook as the angel spoke. This was a terrifying scene. Try to imagine yourself in the picture. What would you do? I would fall to the floor and try to crawl into the nearest crack! It would scare the wits out of me.

Have you ever seen *The Wizard of Oz*? Do you remember when Dorothy, the Scarecrow, Tin Man, and Lion finally got into the Wizard's inner sanctum? A great, booming voice filled the room. Fire and smoke shot heavenward with mighty whooshing sounds. And the four visitors were terrified. Many years ago some of us were watching this movie on television, and I will never forget seeing my young nephew inch slowly into the lap of his father, while other children gaped bug-eyed as the terrifying spectacle unfolded. I have often wondered if the movie producer had read this passage of Isaiah before he envisioned the scene in Oz's throne room.

The reaction of my young nieces and nephews was but a token of the response we would have if we were actually in the temple of God. We would all turn to white Jell-O statues. Isaiah's reaction was "Woe is me!" Why? Because he knew he had sin in his life (I am a man of unclean lips), and the One before him had no sin. He feared that he would die because he was in the presence of the Holy One.

This shows us another characteristic of holiness. Not only does it have no sin, it cannot tolerate sin. It cannot be in the presence of sin. It is untouched by sin and untouchable by sin. There is a great gulf between man and God created by sin. God is holy. We are not. That is, until God works in us. When Isaiah repented of his sin God forgave him, which is symbolized in the hot coal touching his lips. When Isaiah repented and had been forgiven, he was accepted into the presence of God. Furthermore, when God asked "Whom shall I send, and who will go for Us?", Isaiah did not then shrink back from God. His sense of forgiveness took away his fear of being in the presence of this terrifying being. As a result, when Isaiah volunteered, God did not shrink back from Isaiah. Holiness had made the sinner holy and full acceptance followed.

God's Characteristics

God's personal characteristics fall into two categories: those which humanity also possesses, and those which humanity does not possess. The first are often called *moral attributes*, or *communicable attributes* (meaning they can be shared or passed on to others, as in a communicable disease, like the measles). The second are often called *natural attributes*, or *incommunicable attributes* (meaning they cannot be shared or passed on to others, as in incommunicable diseases, such as heart disease, which you cannot "catch" by being around someone with heart disease). God's moral attributes can be summarized:

■ Holiness (God is morally pure, without sin).
■ Love (God desires that which is best for others).
■ Justice (God applies consequences to people's actions according to fixed standards).
■ Goodness (God's will ultimately brings about that which is gratifying, beneficial, and morally upright).

Yes, God is holy. His holiness is a consuming fire (Hebrews 12:29). There is no evil in holiness, and holiness will not tolerate the presence of evil. God, in the end, will therefore destroy all evil, all that is not holy. It is a cause for terror to those who have not been made holy by the work of forgiving grace through faith in Jesus Christ. To those who have, it removes the breach, and therefore the terror. The newly-made holy ones may call the eternal Holy One "Abba," a term of endearment most closely translated "Daddy" (Romans 8:15).

Would you like confirmation of this? Second Corinthians 5:17

says, "if anyone is in Christ, he is a new creation; the old things have passed away; behold, all things have become new." The "old" that has passed away is the old self. Ephesians 4:22 and 24 say, "Lay aside the old self . . . and put on the new self which in the likeness of God has been created in righteousness and holiness of the truth." Your new self has been re-created by God. And having been born again (John 3:3), your new self is holy, just as God is holy.

Of course, this "new self" is still housed in an unchanged body, in which the power of sin still dwells (Romans 7:18–19). But the day will come when your new spiritual self will be joined with a redeemed body, and you will serve the Lord unimpeded by sin (Romans 8:23). In that day, in the fullness of all it means to be a holy creature, you will have full fellowship with a holy God.

Love

When we think of the love of God, it is easy to misunderstand what it means. Love is probably the first positive characteristic which people connect with God, but because it is misunderstood, that is where the ideas such as God being like Santa Claus come from. We hear statements such as, "A loving God would never send anyone to hell." Or, "A loving God would not allow such suffering in the world." Statements like these compel us to go to the Bible, where we will see, for example, that though hell and suffering are real, neither means that God is not love.

Most of us tend to attach a human level of love to God, an emotional, warm, and fuzzy kind of love, because that is our concept of a loving person. When we say, "She is such a loving person," we usually mean that she is warm, giving, and compassionate. God is these things, but He is other things too. All God's characteristics are integrated. He does not exercise one characteristic in isolation from His other characteristics.

There are three words in the original Greek New Testament that translated into English as the one word "love." This often causes some confusion.

- *Eros* is physical, sensual love. We get our word "erotic" from this Greek word. This is not what is meant when the Bible says God is love.
- *Philos* is emotional love, such as one might have for a mother,

father, or close friend. We get our English words philan-
thropist (love of man) and Philadelphia (brotherly love) from
this Greek word. This is not what is meant when the Bible
says God is love.

- *Agape* (pronounced uh-gop'-ay) means to exercise one's will
  for the good of another. We have no common English words
  for it. When the Bible says that God is love, it says that God
  is "agape." This is no "Santa Claus" love. It is the commitment to do good for another person, regardless of whether it
  feels good or is commended by others.

The primary characteristic of agape is that it gives. We see in
John 3:16, "For God so *loved* the world that He *gave*." In Ephesians
5:25, we read, "Husbands, love your wives, just as Christ also
loved the church and *gave* Himself for her."

The agape which God gives to us is beyond comprehension.
The price which God has paid to love humanity is unimaginable.
I heard a story (I was told it was true) in which a little girl needed
a blood transfusion. The only one who had blood compatible
with hers was her younger brother. The young boy's mother and
father asked him if he would be willing to give **God is love.**
his blood to save his sister. He thought about it
gravely for some time and then decided that he would. As he was
lying in the hospital bed, donating a harmless pint of blood, he
looked up to his parents and asked, "When do I die?" He thought
he had to give all his blood and that it would kill him! Yet he was
willing to do it anyway. That is a glimpse of the kind of love God
has for us.

The most obvious sacrifice God made for us is that He sent
His Son Jesus to die for the sins of the world. Jesus came to earth,
took on the form of human flesh as Jesus of Nazareth, lived a life
of dramatic suffering and rejection, which culminated in His being crucified, a particularly cruel form of capital punishment ex-
ercised by the Roman government. That would be bad enough,
but many people were crucified. Jesus was not the only one. In
addition to His life of rejection culminating in His crucifixion, Jesus, at the moment of His death, took on Himself all the sins of the
world. Jesus "bore our sins in His own body on the tree"(1 Peter
2:24). The Crucifixion brought to Jesus an anguish which no human can experience or comprehend. Many theologians and Bible
teachers agree that Jesus outsuffered any human who ever lived.

Many years ago, the U.S.S. *Pueblo*, a ship from the United States Navy, was hijacked by the North Korean military. The incident provoked deep tension worldwide, provoking a diplomatic and military standoff for several days. The eighty-two surviving crew members were thrown into a period of brutal captivity. For example, thirteen of the captured sailors were forced to sit in a rigid manner around a table. After several hours of strict immobility the door was flung open and a North Korean guard brutally beat the sailor in the first chair with the butt of his rifle. The next day, as each sailor sat at his assigned place, again the door was thrown open and the sailor in the first chair was violently beaten. On the third day it happened again to the same man. Knowing the man could not survive, another young sailor took his place. When the door was flung open the guard automatically beat the new victim senseless. For weeks, each day a different sailor stepped forward to sit in that horrible chair, knowing full well what would happen. At last the guards gave up in exasperation. They were unable to beat that kind of sacrificial love.

That is agape. God loves us with that kind of sacrificial love. Each of us was the person sitting in the designated chair until Jesus traded places with us. Thus the Bible says, "But God demonstrates His own love toward us, in that while we were still sinners, Christ died for us" (Romans 5:8).

We may never have to die for someone, or take someone's beating, but 1 Corinthians 13:4–7 describes the kind of sacrificial love we must express to others, as we exemplify God's agape toward us:

> Love suffers long and is kind; love does not envy; love does not parade itself, is not puffed up; does not behave rudely, does not seek its own, is not provoked, thinks no evil; does not rejoice in iniquity, but rejoices in the truth; bears all things, believes all things, hopes all things, endures all things.

As love is the motivating force of God, so, too, it must be for us.

Justice

We don't hear much about God's justice these days. It is not a popular concept because we live in a day when one of our highest values is personal independence. "I don't tell you how to live your life, so don't tell me how to live my life." It is considered highly impolite and unacceptable to stick one's nose into anyone else's business.

Nevertheless, justice is one of God's central characteristics. It can be defined as applying the consequences to a person's actions according to a fixed standard. The fixed standard says that if you do this, then such and such will follow. It is applied consistently to all people, without regard to favoritism or any other intervening thing.

God has said that "all have sinned and fall short of the glory of God" (Romans 3:23), and that the "wages of sin is death" (Romans 6:23). Therefore, God's justice requires that all die. However, His mercy is the characteristic that causes Him to provide the way of escape when we deserve that judgment. We deserve to die, but God **God is just and merciful.** Himself, in Jesus, came to earth and died for us, so that if we believe in Him, and receive Him personally as our Savior, then God will count Jesus' death for ours, and we will receive God's gift of life. This way of escape from that judgment satisfies Him, and when we accept that way of escape, God is not unjust to save us.

When we put God's justice and mercy together, it destroys the two most common misconceptions about God. The first misconception it destroys is that God is a celestial Santa Claus, winking and booming a cheery "Ho, ho, ho!" at our transgressions: "Humans will be humans." Nothing could be further from the truth. He has fixed standards, and violating those standards brings set consequences.

The other misconception it destroys is that God is a harsh, unfeeling judge who is watching from heaven, arms crossed, face in a scowl, just waiting for us to do something wrong so He can zap us with a lightning bolt. Instead of this, He loves us and is exceedingly merciful. He *wants* us to be able to avoid His judgment.

I heard a story, I don't know if it is true, about a young boy who disobeyed his father and was going to receive a spanking. He was taken to his bedroom and instructed to lean over the bed as his father wielded a wooden paddle. As the young boy closed his eyes and waited anxiously for the dreaded blows to fall, he heard the paddle strike but felt nothing. He heard it strike again and again but still did not feel anything. Finally he opened his eyes and saw his father striking himself on the thigh with the paddle as hard as he could. His father had taken the boy's punishment. God's justice and mercy are like that.

Goodness

To do good is one of the most respected things in the world. When one's character is known by the good he has done, that person becomes highly esteemed. We admire people who do good. When we see goodness, it touches us deeply. I remember many years ago reading a quote in a daily devotional magazine that touched me deeply, "We ought always be kind to others, for they may be walking life's road wounded." I thought of all the times I had been unkind to others, not because I meant to, but because I was walking life's road wounded. I resolved to be more kind. This helped me to see God's inherent goodness more clearly, and His intentions toward us.

It is such a wonderful thing that God is good. Think if He were not. There are, and have been, evil gods. These gods are either conjured up in people's minds and then foisted on others, or they may be demons. We have all seen images of the volcano god who demanded the sacrifice of a young virgin each year to appease him so he wouldn't spew his molten vomit all over the village. We have seen the evil looking Hindu gods with many arms and huge, ghastly red tongues gagging from their mouths. We have seen the twisted, grizzly faces of demons personified in carved wood or stone from Africa or other Third World places. In addition, mythology is filled with gods who were imps and tricksters, who were selfish, vindictive, and revengeful. These are bad gods. They do evil things to people. They are unfair. They are inconsistent and unpredictable. It is a wonderful thing that the God of which we speak is good.

But what do we mean by good? "Good" is one of those words like "love"; it is hard to define, though we know it when we see it. It has been God's intention from the beginning of creation to do good. In Genesis 1, God repeatedly calls the things He has created "good" or "very good." He chose Israel out of all the nations of the world and promised to do good for her (Numbers 10:29). He gave Israel commandments "for your good" (Deuteronomy 10:13). David said in Psalm 119:68 that the Lord is good and that everything He does is good. Truly, the Lord is good (2 Chronicles 7:3).

In the New Testament, Jesus calls Himself the Good Shepherd (John 10:14). The apostle Paul wrote in Romans 8:28 that "all things work together for good to those who love God, to those who are the called according to His purpose." Romans 12:1–2 teaches us that God's will is good and perfect. In Philippians 1:6 we read that "He who has begun a good work in you will complete it until the day of Jesus Christ."

As part of His character, God extends that goodness to us. This means that everything God asks of us is for our good. Every piece of instruction, every commandment, and every example is for our good.

The Bible does not define what it means to be good. A dictionary defines it as "having desirable properties, gratifying, enjoyable, beneficial, morally upright." So God has gone on record as saying that His original creation had desirable properties, was gratifying, enjoyable, beneficial and morally upright.

In addition, He intends to extend to His children a gratifying, enjoyable, beneficial, and morally upright experience and relationship with Him. He does this through giving us commands and instructions to follow and by providentially working in our lives. He does this because He Himself is good and all that He touches reflects His goodness. When the Bible says that He intends to do good for His children, it means that He intends to do something for His children that they will ultimately enjoy and benefit . . . and that, forever.

Two extremes must be avoided in understanding the goodness of God. First, it must be understood that God is not out to please only Himself with His creation in a way that harms creation. It is not that God is going to do with humanity what He chooses, even though that **God is good.** might not be good for humans (although such a character and such a notion of "goodness" would not be perfect and thus could not describe God). The only way we can understand the goodness of God is to understand that what He is undertaking to do is desirable from the standpoint of His children. God is not an engineer or scientist fooling around with human toys for His own enjoyment, regardless of the impact on His human toys. Instead God is a caring Creator, as well as the Redeemer and Savior, and we can be sure that His goodness includes "goodness" from his children's point of view.

The second extreme to be avoided is that, when we say God

intends to do good for His children, we mean life will always be easy and pleasurable. We live in a fallen world in which the effects of sin have changed the original game plan. Just as a surgeon must sometimes hurt in order to heal, so God sometimes allows pain into our lives, and then uses it for a good purpose. Being a child of God is not like belonging to Santa Claus, where one can expect unbroken pleasure. God delivers us *through* the pain inherent in a fallen world, but not always *from* it. Suffering is part of the Christian experience. But in the pain, and through the life of sin into which we are all born, God will work good in our lives, and in the end He will usher us into a life of unbroken bliss with Him as He does "good" for us forever.

The above characteristics are not all the ones that God shares with mankind. But they are among the very important ones. We cannot deal with them all without this becoming too large a book. But these are representative of the characteristics which God shares with mankind, and are characteristics which we should appreciate in Him and nurture is our own lives.

Speed Bump!

Slow down to be sure you've gotten the main points in this chapter.

Question Answer

Q1. How do we define God?

A1. God is an infinite, eternal *spirit*, creator of the universe and sovereign over it.

Q2. What characteristics does God share with *humanity*?

A2. Among the characteristics which God shares with humanity are His *moral* characteristics of holiness, love, justice, and goodness.

Fill In the Blank

Question Answer

Q1. How do we define God?

A1. God is an infinite, eternal _____, creator of the universe and sovereign over it.

Q2. What characteristics does God share with _____?

A2. Among the characteristics which God shares with humanity are His _____ characteristics of holiness, love, justice, and goodness.

For Discussion and Thought

1. How did you define God before you read this chapter? Did your definition come from what you understood of the Bible, or did it come from your own internal impression of what you thought God might be like?

2. How important do you think it is to have biblical support for your image of God?

3. How do you think God's possession of His moral attributes differs from our possession of those same attributes? How do the attributes differ between God and us?

4. If a child wanted to know who God is, what would you tell him?

5. How do you think your family experience, educational experience, and other experiences affected your concept of who God is? Do you feel your understanding is better now, or the same?

What if I Don't Believe?

1. It means that my concept of God does not agree with Scripture.

2. It means that I have no way of knowing if my concept of God has any validity. Wishing does not make it so. Just because I might like God to be the way I envision Him, I have no reason to believe that He is actually like that.

3. It means that I have abandoned the biblical and historically accepted concept of who God is, and I am trusting my own instinct to come up with the right answer. It is like rejecting the multiplication tables, and believing (in spite of the fact that there is nothing to believe) that my own inner hunches are correct when I try to multiply numbers.

4. It means that I have rejected the Bible in favor of another religious book, or I have accepted the notion that all truth is relative, and that it is acceptable for each person to decide for himself what God is like.

5. It means that I have no basis for establishing absolute truth; and, as we saw in the last chapter, if there is no God, or if each person can decide for himself what God is like, then all things are permissible. A person

can envision a God who does not care if we murder or rape or steal. A person can envision a God who does not care if we sin at all, and we can be lulled into a false sense of security, which will be shattered when we die and stand face-to-face with a God who did care about those things.

For Further Study

1. Scriptures.

Several Scripture passages speak of who God is and what He is like. They include:

- Luke 7:29; 18:2–7: God is just

- John 3:5–7; 4:23–24: God is spirit

- Romans 8:28; Romans 12:1–2; 3 John 11: God is good

- 1 John 4:7–19: God is love

- Revelation 4 & 5: God is holy

Read these passages and consider how they augment your understanding of who God is.

2. Books.

Several other books are very helpful in studying this subject further. They are listed below in general order of difficulty. If I could read only one of these, I would read the first one:

Know What You Believe, Paul Little
God: Coming Face to Face With His Majesty, John MacArthur
A Survey of Bible Doctrine, Charles Ryrie
Essential Truths of the Christian Faith, R. C. Sproul
Concise Theology, James I. Packer
Knowing God, James I. Packer

The reason the mass of men fear God, and at bottom dislike Him, is because they rather distrust His heart, and fancy Him all brain, like a watch.
■ **Herman Melville**

3

What Is God Like?

In the previous chapter we talked about characteristics which God has that He shares with us. I used the example of a dog my wife and I used to have, Sugar Bear. To me, she was truly amazing. I have owned a number of dogs, but this one by far was the most intelligent. Sugar Bear entered into our life on a level that no other dog ever was able to do. She seemed to understand not only our words but also our thoughts, moods, and body language. All my other dogs were just dogs. She was *Sugar Bear*.

In spite of her intelligence and winsome personality, she did have some quirks. For example, one warm summer evening in the dead of night she began barking incessantly. We lived in the country on seven acres of hardwoods within a larger area of over 100 acres of woods. There were plenty of things for a dog to bark about at night. She would often bark at something unknown for a minute or two, or if there were a slow-moving possum or an arrogant cat she might bark for five or ten minutes. You learned to shut it out. But this night, she must have barked for a half an hour before I finally realized it was out of the ordinary. I had to go find out what was going on if I wanted any more sleep that night!

I stepped out onto the front porch and saw her barking, seemingly into the woods in front of our house. "Sugar Bear, what's wrong?" I wheedled. She came over to be near me, and if I had had a zipper on my body she would have unzipped it and crawled in. She kept barking as we walked toward the driveway. I peered deep into the darkness and saw nothing. As I got closer to the driveway, her barking took on a shrill, near hysterical pitch. She was looking at a pair of boots I inadvertently had left in the driveway. I knelt down at the boots. She was directly behind me now, trying to wake the dead. I picked the boots up and held them toward her and said, "Is this what you are barking at?" As if shot out of a cannon, she turned and sprinted away wildly, yelping and crying as if she were being stung by a thousand bees. I shook my head in utter disbelief, took the boots inside, and went back to a silent night of sleep. Barking at boots!

The boots didn't bother me at all. There were things I knew that Sugar Bear didn't know. There were things utterly mysterious to her that were simple to me. My grasp of the world was so far beyond hers that she would never be able to bridge it. She would never be able to read the newspaper. She would never know the difference between Baroque and Classical music. She would never understand the reasons for the rise and fall of communism. Such things were beyond her, always. But we loved her nevertheless, and she loved us.

In this chapter we learn that . . .

God possesses at least five characteristics that humans do not:

1. God is eternal, existing without a beginning or an end.
2. God is immutable, He has never changed and will never change.
3. God is omnipresent, He is everywhere simultaneously.
4. God is omniscient, He knows all things, both actual and possible.
5. God is omnipotent, He can do whatever He chooses.

There are things about God that are beyond us and there will never be any way to change that. As we saw in the previous chapter, there are some characteristics which we share with God. God is always above us in these characteristics, but we share them to some degree. However, there are certain characteristics that God has which transcend man, and man will never possess them. We want to look at those characteristics in this chapter.

Does God Have a Beginning and an End?

God is eternal, existing without a beginning or an end.

When I was about junior high age, I went through a time in which I did not go to sleep easily at night. I would lie awake as my mind wandered to imponderable subjects. I used to think a lot about infinity of distance. I used to imagine the infinite distance that I thought existed in the universe. If you went straight up for a million, billion, trillion, quadrillion miles into the universe and came to a brick wall, all you would have to do is crawl over the brick wall and keep going to realize that you had only begun. There was, and could be, I reasoned, no end to space. Or if space ended and something else was there, there could be no end to it. There could be no end to distance. Whenever you thought you were at the end of "distance," there was always something on the other side. My mind would reel at the impossibility, and yet necessity, of such a thought. Such thoughts would begin to unnerve me, even frighten me a little, and I would deliberately pull back mentally. I didn't understand why my thoughts frightened me, but the closer I came to feeling that I was grasping infinity of distance, the more frightened I got.

I would also think about eternity of time. I had no difficulty starting with a fixed point in time, like my birthday, and going on forever. Time, like distance, could not end. But what I had great difficulty with was to go back- **God is eternal.** ward and realize that time could have no beginning. That really freaked me out. No end to time in the future I could handle, but no beginning—that was too much. I couldn't handle it. I would get frightened and pull back.

My mind was just as capable of understanding those matters then as it is now. But I realize now that, in a figurative sense, my finite mind was reaching out and touching the infinite mind of God, and I was not capable of mastering the moment. My reach exceeded my grasp. As if shot out of a cannon, I turned, yelping and crying as though I were being stung by a thousand bees.

Though I had never been instructed in theology, my mind was, instinctively, rubbing shoulders with one of the great characteristics of God: He has no end. That, I have no trouble with. But He has no beginning—it can't be. But it must be.

Where did everything come from? Scientists say it came from a big ball of mud bubbling in the center of the universe which eventually exploded and formed the galaxies we see today. My mind asks, "Where did the mud come from?" Scientists say, "The mud just always was." I don't buy it. Others suggest that the mud wasn't always there, but came into existence somehow. I don't buy that either. Something coming from nothing? It is easier to believe in God than to believe that something came from nothing. The scientist will then say, "Well, if you believe in God, where did God come from?" But that question is absurd. There must be a beginning point. The beginning point can either be an eternal ball of mud, or it can be an eternal God. It takes more faith to believe in the ball of mud than it does to believe in God. God is eternal. He never had a beginning, and He will never have an end (Psalm 90:2). It is a very reassuring thought to me. It makes me feel safe. The universe can make sense to me. He always has been, and He always will be, and I am safe, loved, and significant.

Does God Ever Change?

God is immutable, He has never changed and will never change.

Another important characteristic of God is that He never changes (Hebrews 13:8). Theologians call this characteristic "immutability," which Webster defines simply as "unchanging." All change must be for the better or for the worse. If God is perfect, He could not change for the better. You cannot improve on perfection. And, if He is perfect, He cannot change for the worse for the same reason. If God ever changed, or ever could change, we could never be sure of anything. So God loves us today! So what? If He could change, He might not love us tomorrow.

God cannot change because His very nature is unchanging. Therefore, He can never be wiser, more holy, more just, more merciful, more truthful; nor less. Nor do His plans **God is immutable.** and purposes change. He is the same yesterday, today, and forever. The apostle James writes that God is "the Father of lights, with whom there is no variation or shadow of turning" (James 1:17). Malachi writes that "I am the Lord, I do not change" (Malachi 3:6).

A contradiction seems to come when we read a passage such as Numbers 23:19, which says that God does not repent (change His mind), and a passage such as Exodus 32:14, which says that God changed His mind. However, it can be resolved fairly easily. It is precisely because God is unchanging in His moral character that evokes different responses from Him when people themselves change their minds. In Jeremiah 18:7–10, we read:

> The instant I speak concerning a nation and concerning a kingdom, to pluck up, to pull down, and to destroy it, if that nation against whom I have spoken turns from its evil, I will relent of the disaster that I thought to bring upon it.

So it is not inconsistent for God to change His mind and refrain from judgment when a nation repents. His specific actions might change, but His nature, character, and purposes do not.

Is God Everywhere?

God is omnipresent, He is everywhere simultaneously.

The next three characteristics form a well-known triad, each one beginning with the syllable "omni," which means "unlimited." (If you are omnivorous, it means you will eat anything.) The first one is "omnipresence," meaning that God is everywhere present simultaneously. In Psalm 139:7–10 we read, "Where can I go from Your Spirit? Or where can I flee from Your presence? If I ascend into heaven, You are there; if I make my bed in hell, behold, You are there. If I take the wings of the morning, and dwell in the uttermost parts of the sea, even there Your hand shall lead me, and Your right hand shall hold me."

There is nowhere we can go and not be in the presence of God. As Paul Little has observed in his book *Know What You Believe*, "He is not like a substance spread out in a thin layer all over the earth—all of Him is in Chicago, in Calcutta, in Cairo, and in Caracas, at one and the same time."

Now there are some important implications to omnipresence. One is that omnipresence is not pantheism. Omnipresence states that God is everywhere. Pantheism states that everything is God, or a part of God. If you were **God is omnipresent.** sitting in a tree, omnipresence says that God is present with you. Pantheism states that the tree is God. The God of the Bible, however, is separate and distinct from His creation, though He is present with it.

Second, omnipresence means that you cannot sin without sinning in the presence of God. If you are tempted to tell a little white lie to someone you don't know, God is present. If you are tempted to commit a sexual sin with another person, God is there. If you are tempted to falsify your income tax report in the privacy of your own study, God is there. You cannot sin without sinning in the presence of God.

Third, omnipresence means that God is always with you. You

are not alone. Loneliness is one of the greatest emotional problems of the day. Billy Graham has stated that when he preaches on loneliness, he gets a greater response than on any other topic. Because God is omnipresent, the person who is alone or lonely can take comfort from that. God is there. Many reports of prisoners of war and hostages, who have spent many years isolated, have reported that knowing that God was present sustained their faith.

Does God Know Everything?

God is omniscient, He knows all things, both actual and possible.

I have flown quite a bit in the last twenty years. I like to get to the airport with five minutes to spare. My idea of a perfect arrival is to be let off at the curb, check my luggage, walk briskly to the gate just as they are ready to close the door on the plane. This drives many people crazy. My mother-in-law is a careful flyer. She likes to arrive at least one hour ahead of time, to make sure that if you have a flat tire on the way you will still make your flight. Hers is the more prudent way, but I couldn't do it if my life depended on it. And it has been my observation that early arrivers miss as many planes as late arrivers. I have missed only one plane because of a purely late arrival. I have missed another plane because the airport people mover system broke down while I was in it. I missed another plane because I was reading the sports section of the San Francisco newspaper in a remote section of the airport while I had a two-hour layover. Dumb. Expensive.

My most mind-boggling experience came several years ago when I was living in Austin, Texas. I was flying to Atlanta through Dallas. My American Airlines flight left Austin for Dallas at 6:30 A.M., and left Dallas for Atlanta at 8:30 A.M. In Austin, I walked in a sleepy blur to the gate that said Dallas, 6:30 A.M. The flight attendant looked at my boarding pass and invited me to board. I settled in for what I knew would be at least thirty more minutes of sleep. We landed, and as I got off of the plane the red-jacketed man meeting the flight asked me if I had a connecting flight. I said I did, flight 1242.

"Sir, we have no flight 1242," the man said.

"Of course you do," I said, and showed him my ticket.

"Sir, that's an *American Airlines* ticket."

I blinked hard. "Who are you?" I asked thickly.

"Delta," he replied.

I stared at him blankly. On the outside I was the picture of sober control and decorum, but inside my mind was screaming, *"Delta? How in the world could you be Delta? I flew American! Where am I? Who am I? What has happened?"* My mind raced for some snatch of meaning. I felt as though I were in the Twilight Zone. Eventually I was able to speak.

"How did I get here?"

"Sir, I have no idea."

"Where is this?"

"Dallas, sir."

Dallas. At least I'm at the right airport. N-No need to p-panic. All I have to do is take the people mover to the American terminal, which I have enough time to do, and take my flight to Atlanta. Everything is okay. Everything is okay. Everything is okay.

I got on my American Airlines flight to Atlanta, but for the life of me I have a hard time figuring out what happened. The best I can guess is that both American Airlines *and* Delta had flights leaving Austin for Dallas at 6:30 that morning, and that the gates were right next to each other. By the time I arrived, everyone else was on board, they were in a hurry, and the flight attendant did not check my boarding pass carefully enough. In the providence of God, the plane was going to Dallas and not Singapore!

I have often thought of that incident. I was one person in one place at one point in time, in a circumstance in which there are many safeguards built in, and *still*, something went wrong. Can you imagine what the world would be like if God did not know everything? We'd all be in Singapore!

God's "Omni" Attributes

omni = unlimited

*omni*present = unlimited presence. God is everywhere simultaneously.

*omni*scient (knowledge) = unlimited knowledge. God knows all things both actual and possible.

*omni*potent (power) = unlimited power. God is able to do whatever He chooses.

The second "omni" characteristic of God is His "omni-science," which means that God knows everything, both actual and possible. Psalm 139:4 reads, "For there is not a word on my tongue, but behold, O LORD, You know it altogether." When we say God knows everything, we mean that He knows all things, both actual and possible. In Matthew 11:21, Jesus said, "If the mighty works which were done in you had been done in Tyre and Sidon, they would have repented long ago in sackcloth and ashes."

God is omniscient.

God knows everything about everything. "The very hairs of your head are all numbered," Jesus said (Luke 12:7). Not even one sparrow is forgotten by God (Luke 12:6). God even knows our thoughts and intents (Heb. 4:12).

The implications of God's omniscience are similar to the implications for His omnipresence. First, it is a comfort to His children. No piece of information that God needs to keep his children safe will escape His notice. No knowledge needed to correct a mishap or solve a problem is missing. Do you hurt? God knows. Are you lonely? God knows. Are you confused? God knows. Do you have need? God knows. And even though He knows our every thought, He still loves us. The apostle Paul wrote, God "demonstrates His own love toward us, in that while we were still sinners, Christ died for us" (Romans 5:8). Every sin we would ever commit was in the future when Christ died for us, and yet He died for us anyway. Take heart. God knows, and He loves us anyway.

On the other side of the ledger, there is no hoodwinking God. There is no wool to be pulled over His eyes. Jeremiah wrote, "I, the LORD, search the heart, I test the mind, even to give every man according to his ways, according to the fruit of his doings (Jeremiah 17:10). Here is the futility of trying to hide sin from God. We've got the spotlights at Carnegie Hall trained on us. Hypocrisy is ludicrous. Sneaking is ridiculous. Are you trying to put one over on God? Think again. One who is omniscient has nothing put over on Him.

The philosopher Seneca once wrote, "I will govern my life and thoughts as if the whole world were to see the one and read the other, for what does it signify to make anything a secret to my neighbor, when to God, who is the searcher of our hearts, all our privacies are open?"

Can God Do Anything He Wants?

God is omnipotent, He can do whatever He chooses.

The final "omni" characteristic of God is His power. Omnipotence means that God can do anything He chooses. Job 42:2 reads, "I know that You can do everything, and that no purpose of Yours can be withheld from You." **God is omnipotent.** He put the galaxies in place. He breathed life into a lump of clay and created man.

It is by looking at nature, and specifically "space," that we get some feel for God's omnipotence. An article from *National Geographic* speaks well to this subject:

Far from the land of everyday, out in the distant curves of the universe, lie strange and fantastic realms, unlike anything in our wildest dreams. Hidden by the barriers of time and space, they have lived forever beyond the reach of man, unknown and unexplored.

But now, just now, the cosmic barriers have begun to lift a little. Man has had his first glimpses of these once secret domains, and their bizarre ways have left him stunned. They challenge his very notions of matter and energy. With Alice in Wonderland, he says, "One *can't* believe impossible things."

And impossible, indeed, they seem to be. In those far reaches of the universe, in those bewildering worlds, are far places . . .

- Where a teaspoon of matter weighs as much as 200 million elephants . . .
- Where a tiny whirling star winks on and off thirty times a second . . .
- Where a small mysterious object shines with the brilliance of ten trillion suns . . .
- Where matter and light are continually sucked up by devouring black holes, never to be seen again.

Small wonder the late British scientist J. B. S. Haldane could say, "The universe is not only queerer than we suppose, but queerer than we *can* suppose."

We used to think that the universe was simply our Milky Way Galaxy. Today we know that galaxies are as common as blades of grass in a meadow. They number perhaps a hundred billion.

How does one comprehend the incredible size of this galaxy-filled universe? For such awesome distances, scientists and astronomers think in terms of time, and they use the telescope as a time machine. They measure space by a unit called the light-year, the distance light travels in one year at the rate of 186,282 miles per second — about six trillion miles ("The Incredible Universe" 589).

Conclusion

"Knowing God" begins with believing the truth about Him. If we doubt one of these characteristics, we erode our basis for knowing God. We begin by accepting that these things are true of God. He is loving. He is just. He is merciful. He is all powerful. He is all knowing. He is present everywhere. He has no beginning or end. Accepting the truth of what we know about God is the first step in knowing Him intimately. We learn to know God intimately as we come to see Him act consistently and predictably with these characteristics.

Why Do I Need to Know About God's Unique Characteristics?

1. If God is not eternal, it means He is not the final answer for the existence of the universe. There is something greater than God.
2. If God is not unchangeable, then He might tell us one thing and do another.
3. If God is not omnipresent, then we might end up in trouble, and God would not be there to help.
4. If God is not omniscient, then He might be ignorant of something terribly important.
5. If God is not omnipotent, then He might want to do something we need but not be able to. God may be loving, kind, and merciful, as we saw in the last chapter but not be able to do anything about it. These unique characteristics are crucial if God is to be God.

If we truly believed these things about God, it would radically change our attitude and behavior toward Him. We are warmed by these thoughts as we read about them or hear them preached on Sunday morning, but let Monday morning come and there is a distinct shift in our thinking. We find a memo in our box that someone younger, with less seniority in the company, has just been promoted ahead of us. We are now going to be working for that young little jerk who isn't even dry behind the ears. Our stomach is pumped full of acid, our bloodstream is injected with bile, and our heart starts pounding from adrenaline. We are angry and we are hurt. We're disappointed and frankly, a little scared. So where is God? Where is the steady direction of His will toward my welfare? That nice little homily suddenly seems cold, distant, and unrelated to the real world. Merciful, is He? Does He know about the little twerp I'm going to have to work for now? Omniscient? Did He know this was coming? Omnipotent? Was He able to do anything about it? Love? Does He care about this situation?

You see, the problem isn't that we have trouble understanding the attributes of God. It is that we have trouble reconciling them with the real world, with our experience and observation. If God is good, what happened to my job, my marriage, my kids? What is happening to my health, my finances, my friends?

Sure, we can understand the *concepts* of love, mercy, omnipotence and omniscience. They just don't seem to be present in the world we live in. So how do we put these characteristics into our life Monday morning? What does God have to say about that?

If the Holy Spirit were able to speak audibly to you, I think He might say something like:

> For what credit is it if, when you are beaten for your faults, you take it patiently? But when you do good and suffer, if you take it patiently, this is commendable before God. For to this you were called, because Christ also suffered for us, leaving us an example, that you should follow His steps; who committed no sin, nor was deceit found in His mouth; who, when He was reviled, did not revile in return; while He suffered, He did not threaten, but committed Himself to Him who judges righteously (1 Peter 2:20–23).

> Beloved, do not think it strange concerning the fiery trial which is to try you, as though some strange thing happened to you; but rejoice to the extent that you partake of Christ's sufferings, that when His glory is revealed, you may also be glad with exceeding joy (1 Peter 4:12–13).

> Before I was afflicted, I went astray, but now I keep Your word. It is good for me that I have been afflicted, that I may learn Your statutes. I know, O Lord, that Your judgments are right,

and that in faithfulness You have afflicted me (Psalm 119:67, 71, 75).

The sufferings of this present time are not worthy to be compared with the glory which shall be revealed in us. (Romans 8:18)

Therefore we do not lose heart, even though our outward man is perishing, yet the inward man is being renewed day by day. For our light affliction, which is but for a moment, is working for us a far more exceeding and eternal weight of glory, while we do not look at the things which are seen, but at the things which are not seen. For the things which are seen are temporary, but the things which are not seen are eternal (2 Corinthians 4:17–18).

In other words, "I promised you a rose garden in the next life, and enough grace for the thorns in this life. I promised you that, if you would dedicate your life to me totally, and live for my values, I would use you significantly in ministry to others and would fill your life with peace, love and joy. The problem is that you are living for this world, and you feel that I am here to make your life comfortable in this world, and I have failed you if I don't give you the things you want in this world. You have things backward. You are to serve Me. I am not to serve you."

We grind and chafe and labor through the things of this life because we have many things backward. We own nothing. We are owed nothing by God. Our payoff is not in this life. We have a job to do here. That is to manifest the character and proclaim the name of Jesus in this life . . . to help as many others to go to heaven as possible. We have a short-term objective. We can settle down and get comfortable later.

When we live for ourselves in this life, we are miserable and unfulfilled, even when we get many of the things we want. When we give up on this life and live for the next, we have peace and love and joy even when we don't get the things we would like to have.

God loves us. Always. He always directs His purposes for our welfare. He never varies from that. He is merciful. He is omnipotent. He is omniscient. He is omnipresent. It is just that, from time to time, we forget where we are. We are not home yet. We are visitors in this world.

I read one time of a missionary couple who had spent their entire lives in the Central African Republic, working with medical missions among the nationals. They also taught them to read, as well as farming, building, and social and cultural skills. When they retired, they sailed home on a large passenger ship. It just so happened that Teddy Roosevelt had been in Africa on one of his famous safaris, and as the ship docked in New York harbor there was a band playing, crowds cheering, confetti flying, and banners waving. All this hoopla over a President returning from a hunting trip.

"It's not fair," thought the missionary. "The president goes hunting, is gone for a few weeks, and when he comes home, he receives a hero's welcome. We spend our entire lives in an under-developed country, forsaking comfort and recognition for the cause of Christ, and when we come home there isn't even anyone at the dock to meet us."

Suddenly insight from the Holy Spirit flashed into his mind. "Ah, yes. But the difference is, you are not home yet."

You will be treated poorly in this life. You will not get the reward that is due you. That doesn't change one thing about who God is. It only means that you are not home yet. So, "be steadfast, immovable, always abounding in the work of the Lord, knowing that your labor is not in vain in the Lord" (1 Corinthians 15:58).

Speed Bump!

Slow down to be sure you've gotten the main points of this chapter.

Question Answer

Q1. Does God have a beginning and an end?

A1. God is *eternal*, existing without a beginning or an end.

Q2. Does God ever change?

A2. God is *immutable*, He has never changed and will never change.

Q3. Is God everywhere?

A3. God is *omnipresent*, He is everywhere simultaneously.

Q4. Does God know everything?

A4. God is *omniscient*, He knows all things, both actual and possible.

Q5. Can God do anything He wants?

A5. God is *omnipotent*, He can do whatever He chooses.

Fill In the Blank

Question
Answer

Q1. Does God have a beginning and an end?

A1. God is _____, existing without a beginning or an end.

Q2. Does God ever change?

A2. God is _____; He has never changed and will never change.

Q3. Is God everywhere?

A3. God is _____; He is everywhere simultaneously.

Q4. Does God know everything?

A4. God is _____; He knows all things, both actual and possible.

Q5. Can God do anything He wants?

A5. God is _____; He can do whatever He chooses.

For Discussion and Thought

1. Either as a child or as an adult, have you ever pondered the eternality and infinity of God? What were some of your thoughts and feelings?

2. What would you think God to be if He did not possess the unique characteristics described in this chapter?

3. If a child wanted to know what God is like, what would you say?

4. Were you aware of these characteristics of God before reading this chapter? Has your concept of God changed any as a result of reading it?

What If I Don't Believe?

1. You are turning your back on the clearly revealed information about God in the Bible, or else thinking that the Bible isn't true.

2. You have either no God or a small God who cannot come to your rescue, either in this life or the life to come.

3. You have no hope. You must make it through life on your own resources, because a God who lacks power, knowledge, presence, stability, and eternality may sympathize with your problems but cannot help you with them.

For Further Study

1. Scriptures.

- Psalm 90:2; Genesis 21:33: God is eternal

- Hebrews 13:8; James 1:17: God is immutable

- Jeremiah 23:24; Psalm 139:7–10: God is omnipresent

- Matthew 11:21; Psalm 139:2; John 2:25: God is omniscient

- Job 42:2; Psalm 135:5–6: God is omnipotent

Read these passages and consider how they expand your understanding of God.

2. Books.

There are several other helpful books for studying this subject further. They are listed below in general order of difficulty. If I could only read one of these, I would read the first one:

Know What You Believe, Paul Little
God: Coming Face to Face With His Majesty, John MacArthur
A Survey of Bible Doctrine, Charles Ryrie
Concise Theology, James I. Packer
Knowing God, James I. Packer

Tell me how it is that in this room there are
three candles and but one light, and I will
explain to you the [Trinity].
■ John Wesley

4

What Is the Trinity?

In Lewis Carroll's *Alice Through the Looking Glass*, Alice is asked to believe something that is impossible. Alice replies, "One can't believe impossible things!" The White Queen replied that of course one could believe impossible things if one simply tried hard enough. She, herself, had made it a habit of believing six impossible things each day before breakfast.

The doctrine of the Trinity is one of the central teachings of Christianity, and yet it is one of the most difficult to understand, for the reason that it seems impossible. Simply stated, it says that God is one Being yet three persons. Even to write it, or to read it, one stumbles over the mathematics of it. If something is one, how can it be three? If something is three, how can it be one? It seems like saying that something is wet and yet dry, or hot and yet cold. If something is one thing, how can it be its opposite? If something is singular, how can it also be plural?

Thomas Jefferson was a towering intellect, one of the most highly regarded minds in history. In testimony to that, President John Kennedy, shortly after he was elected, gathered some of the most brilliant minds in America to help him forge his approach to governing the United States. At a state dinner with them, President Kennedy said, "This is the most impressive concentration of intelligence ever assembled at a White House dinner, with the possible exception of when Mr. Jefferson dined here alone." Jefferson, even with his massive intellect, struggled with the Trinity. He once wrote:

When we shall have done away with the incomprehensible jargon of the Trinitarian arithmetic, that three are one, and one is three; when we shall have knocked down the artificial scaffolding, reared to mask from view the very simple structure of Jesus; when, in short, we shall have unlearned everything which has been taught since his day, and got back to the pure and simple doctrines he inculcated, we shall then be truly and worthily his disciples. (quoted in *Understanding the Trinity* 110)

Nevertheless, the doctrine of the Trinity has stood for centuries and is stoutly defended as one of the fundamentals of the faith. Where did the doctrine come from? Why are we asked to believe something so seemingly contradictory? Asked with the right spirit, these are honest and appropriate questions. Truth need never fear examination.

The word "trinity" never occurs in the Bible, but we come to the conclusion of the Trinity simply by trying to be faithful to the Bible, which is the Word of God.

In this chapter we learn that . . . .

1. God is one, but His oneness is complex, not simple.
2. The Father, the Son, and the Holy Spirit are each God.
3. The Father, the Son, and the Holy Spirit are distinct persons within the one being of God.

The Bible says that there is only one God. This is particularly consistent in the Old Testament, though it is reiterated in the New. Yet the New Testament calls Jesus God and calls the Holy Spirit God. The doctrine of the Trinity is simply an effort put these statements together. No one started out saying, "I think we need an incomprehensible and unexplainable doctrine." Rather, any reader can see that the Bible teaches, with convincing clarity, that God is three and yet one.

So what do we do with that? The bottom line is that we must either hold to the doctrine of the Trinity, or begin whacking things out of our Bibles. If you think that is extreme, it is exactly what Thomas Jefferson did. He created his own version of the Bible by cutting out what he didn't think belonged there and pasting together what he thought did, coming up with the "Jeffersonian" Bible. It is a grand example of making "reason" god and God unreasonable. So, if we are not prepared to begin whacking things out of our Bible, how do we arrive at the doctrine of the Trinity?

How Many Gods Does the Bible Teach There Are?

The Bible teaches that there is only one God.

That there is only one God is a teaching heavily emphasized in the Old Testament. The message of God's unity was elevated in a time and place when many gods were recognized by those who were not Jews. For the most part, these gods were abominable deities, promoting immorality, self-indulgence, and profound cruelty as a basis for appeasement. There were three gods who had particularly high profiles, and who were especially odious to the true God, Jehovah.

Baal means "master." He was the "sun god," the most important god worshipped by the Canaanites (those who lived in the Promised Land before and after the Israelites took up residence there after their captivity in Egypt). He was the god of fer-

---

Gods of Ancient Israel's Neighbors

Three popular false gods widely worshipped in the Middle East during Old Testament times were:

1. *Baal, the Canaanite sun god of fertility.* Canaan corresponds with modern-day Israel. Canaanites lived there until Israel became a nation. Some Canaanite people lived there even after that and kept alive the dreadful worship of Baal.
2. *Ashtaroth, the Phoenician goddess of fertility, the female partner of Baal.* Phoenicia was a country just north of Israel near modern-day Lebanon.
3. *Molech, the national god of the Ammonites who demanded child sacrifice.* Ammon generally corresponds with modern-day Jordan whose capital city is Amman.

---

tility, worshipped extensively in western Asia from Babylonia to Egypt. In the Old Testament his worship rivaled that of Jehovah and seems to have reached its height in Israel during the days of King Ahab and Jezebel (1 Kings 16–22). People who followed this god engaged in drunken sexual orgies as a way of worshiping him and invoking his blessing on their personal fertility. Altars were built in high places as centers for Baal worship, which was accompanied not only by drunken orgies but at times by the live sacrifice of children.

Ashtaroth was a Phoenician goddess similar to Baal, except

that Baal was male. They were closely associated, and altars to Baal often accompanied an idol of Ashtaroth, suggesting that she was Baal's female partner.

Third was Molech, a particularly foul god of the Ammonites whose primary form of worship involved the burning of live children to him. These gods were so evil, it is not hard to see why Paul said that the "other gods" people worshipped were actually demons (1 Corinthians 10:20).

In this polytheistic content, it is understandable that the Old Testament emphasized that there was only one true God, and that He alone was to be wor- **God is one.** shipped. Thus God issued the first of His Ten Commandments: "You shall have no other gods before Me" (Exodus 20:3). Forty years later, by the inspiration of God, Moses declared, "Hear, O Israel: The LORD our God, the LORD is one! You shall love the LORD your God with all your heart, with all your soul, and with all your strength" (Deuteronomy 6:4–5).

The truth is affirmed in the New Testament. "We know that an idol is nothing in the world, and that there is no other God but one" (1 Corinthians 8:4). "[There is] one God and Father of all, who is above all, and through all, and in you all" (Ephesians 4:6). "You believe that there is one God. You do well" (James 2:19).

Both the Old and the New Testaments, therefore, state that there is only one true God.

Who Are Jesus and the Holy Spirit?

In addition to God the Father, Jesus and the Holy Spirit are also called God in the Bible.

As we said, nowhere does the Bible use the term "Trinity." We get the idea from what the Bible says about the Father, Jesus, and the Holy Spirit.

First, we reiterate what is rarely debated, that the Father is God. The apostle John, recording the words of Jesus, says, "Do not labor for the food which perishes, but for the food which endures to everlasting life, **God is tri-unity,** which the Son of Man will give you, because **three "persons" in** God *the Father* has set His seal on Him" (John **one Being.** 6:27). Peter supports this when he mentions *"God the Father"* in 1 Peter 1:2. Few have difficulty with that.

But Jesus is also recognized as God in the New Testament.

Jesus appeared to some of His disciples after his crucifixion and resurrection. However, Thomas (forever dubbed "Doubting Thomas" for his skeptical attitude) questioned the reality of their report. He stoutly declared that he would not believe unless he were able to put his fingers into Jesus' wounds. Strong words. I don't think he ever thought he would have to eat them. In a magnanimous gesture of accommodation, Jesus appeared to Thomas and said, "Reach your finger here, and look at My hands; and reach your hand here, and put it into My side. Do not be unbelieving, but believing." Thomas then answered Jesus with, "My Lord and my God!" (John 20:27–28). What a gracious act of kindness for Jesus to have done that. For the sake of one man who expressed not cynicism, but honest reservation, Jesus went the extra mile to win him over. He does that with anyone who expresses honest questions, in a desire, not to reject the truth, but to know it.

Apart from clear testimony as to who He was, Jesus did and said things that can be interpreted only as divine. In a remarkable passage in Mark 2:1–12, Jesus was teaching in a home so crowded that no one else could get in. As a result, the friends of a paralytic man began tearing off the roof of the house to let him down by Jesus to be healed. It wasn't difficult to spot the faith behind their dramatic actions. Jesus said to the paralytic man, "My son, your

Jesus spoke and acted as God.

sins are forgiven." With this, the religious leaders went ballistic. Heads jerked. Veins popped. Jaws went slack. What had they heard? This was blasphemy! No one can forgive sins but God! Knowing their thoughts, Jesus said, "Which is easier, to say to the paralytic, 'Your sins are forgiven you,' or to say 'Arise, take up your bed and walk'?"

The answer is, of course, it is easier to say "Your sins are forgiven you." Who is going to prove you wrong for such an unobservable phenomenon? So to prove that He acted with God's full authority, Jesus said, "Arise, take up your bed and walk." The point Jesus was making was, if He could heal a man of paralysis it would indicate that He could forgive sin, which would imply that He was God.

Jesus' words also betrayed that He was God. In John 8, Jesus was debating religious leaders who were looking for reasons to reject Him. They were arguing about whether Jesus was old enough to have seen Abraham, the father of all Jews who had lived two thousand years earlier. When Jesus said to them, "Most assuredly, I say to you, before Abraham was, I AM," the Jews picked up stones to throw at Him.

Why did they do that? Wasn't that an overreaction? Jesus was only off on His chronology by a couple of thousand years. Is that any reason to stone a man? The reason they tried to stone Him was because God's name, revealed to Moses in Exodus 3:14 and revered by devout Jews in Jesus' day, is "I AM." When Jesus, therefore, said, "I AM," the Jews knew He was claiming to be God. And to them, this was blasphemy. The penalty for blaspheming God was death by stoning. This conflict concerned no little chronological computing error. Jesus' identifying Himself as I AM drew a line in the sand, and the Jews either had to accept Jesus or reject Him. They rejected Him (John 8:58–59).

A similar event occurred in John 10:30–33, where Jesus said, "I and My Father are one." When the Jews took up stones to stone Him, Jesus asked, "For which of [my good] works do you stone me?" And the Jews replied, "For a good work we do not stone You, but for blasphemy, and because You, being a man, make Yourself God."

Make no mistake. The Jews understood the significance of Jesus' deeds and words. They knew He was claiming to be God.

Finally, we come to the Holy Spirit. The Bible also presents Him, unambiguously, as God. Early on in the Acts of the Apostles, many of the first Christians in Jerusalem were living in a communal situation, probably because of the persecution of Christians which sprang up with the crucifixion of Jesus. Also, the newness of what was happening, all the excitement, miracles and explosive growth created an environment which made people want to stay together for the experience of it all. Many Jews who were there actually lived elsewhere, and had come to Jerusalem for the Passover, and had not yet gone back home.

To survive, many people who had possessions sold them, and brought the money to the apostles to use for the need of the whole. A man named Joseph sold some property and brought the money from the sale and laid it at the apostles' feet.

Perhaps this seemed like an extraordinary gesture of generosity which made Joseph look very spiritual in the eyes of the new Christian community. In this context, a husband and wife named Ananias and Sapphira sold some real estate which they owned, kept some of the money for themselves, and brought the rest to the apostles. They must have made some kind of a statement or pretense when they gave the money, which led the people to believe that they have given all the money from the sale of the property. Either God or someone else let Peter know that they had not given all the money from the sale, and they misrepresented the facts. Peter called them on it. Paraphrasing, he said, "Ananias, why has Satan filled your heart to lie to the Holy Spirit, and to keep back some of the price of the land? No one forced you to sell the property, did they? And after you sold it, no one forced you to give even a thin dime to us. Yet, you have made it appear as though you gave all the money." Then he said, "You have not lied to men, but to God." In this passage, Peter equated lying to the Holy Spirit as lying to God. Also, the Holy Spirit has the same attributes as God, such as omniscience (1 Corinthians 2:10) and omnipresence (Psalm 139:7). He also existed before the creation of the world and participated in the creation (Genesis 1:2), along with God the Father and Jesus (Colossians 1:15–16).

And the Father, Son, and Holy Spirit are linked together in several key New Testament passages. In 2 Corinthians 13:13–14, Paul writes a benediction which includes all three: "The grace of the Lord Jesus Christ, and the love of God, and the communion of the Holy Spirit be with you all." If Jesus and the Holy Spirit were not God, Paul would be presumptuous, indeed, to link them as equal with the Father. And there is the Trinitarian prayer for grace and peace from the Father, the Spirit, and Jesus Christ in Revelation 1:4–5. In the Trinitarian benediction, we see the Father mentioned first, the Son second, and the Spirit third. In the Revelation passage, we see the Father first, the Spirit second, and the Son third. This capacity to alter the order of persons reinforces their equality in the minds of the inspired writers of Scripture.

The Bible presents the Holy Spirit as God.

In Matthew 28:19, Jesus instructs the disciples to go and make disciples of all the nations, "baptizing them in the name [not names!] of the Father and of the Son and of the Holy Spirit." "These three persons are the one God to whom Christians commit themselves" (J.I. Packer, *Concise Theology*, 41).

And we also find the Trinity present at Jesus'baptism. Jesus is in the water, God the Father speaks from heaven, and the Holy Spirit descends on Jesus in the visible form of a dove (Mark 1:9–11).

Again, the Bible never uses the word "Trinity" or says that

"God is three and yet one." However, Trinitarian faith and thinking are found throughout the Bible, and in that sense "Trinity" is sound doctrine.

Can the Doctrine of the Trinity Be Fully Explained?

Attempts to explain the doctrine of the Trinity fully fall short, as do all attempts to explain God fully. The statements of Scripture that form this doctrine must be taken by faith at face value.

What do you do with this information? How do you reconcile the fact that the Old Testament seems very clear that God is one, supported by key passages in the New Testament, and yet, in the New Testament, we see the Son and the Spirit being presented as having the same attributes as the Father and linked with the Father in apparent equality in two key passages?

The doctrine of the Trinity did not come first and the passages second. The passages came first, and the doctrine of the Trinity came as the best effort of devout, cautious, and thoughtful believers to harmonize the passages. I confess, I see no other solution to the passages than the historical doctrine of the Trinity.

An attempt to explain only the oneness destroys the threeness, and an attempt to explain only the threeness destroys the oneness. So what do we do? We have three choices. One, we can start whacking away at our Bibles as Thomas Jefferson did, setting ourselves up as the judge as to what is acceptable and unacceptable in the Bible. Or, like the White Queen, we can believe impossible things. We can say, God is full of nonsense, but I believe it anyway. Or, we can admit that while we cannot fully understand it, it makes sense to God and will make sense to us when we stand before God. For now we choose to believe it even though it transcends our understanding.

The first option is mischievous because if you don't believe the entire Bible, where do you stop believing? With the Trinity? With the virgin birth of Christ? With a literal, bodily resurrection? Where do you stop? Deciding you are the judge over the Bible is like scooting off the top of an Olympic ski jump. There is no place to stop. Who knows enough to tinker with the Word of God? Because the Bible is God's book, I would rather place my confidence in it completely than I would Thomas Jefferson's judgment, or my own judgment, or anyone else's. Denominations and parachurch organizations that started out selecting what they would believe and not believe in the Bible end up believing almost nothing of it.

Choosing the second option is to give ourselves over to nonsense. People who do this end up with a meaningless Bible.

The third option makes sense. Physicist Stephen Hawking, who is terribly disabled, lives in a wheelchair, and can barely communicate, has written a book entitled *A Brief History of Time*. He is considered by some to be the greatest scientific mind since Albert Einstein. His book was on the *New York Times* Best Seller list for an impressive length of time for a book of that kind. But few people really understood it, requiring a second book to be written explaining the first one. If Stephen Hawking says things that go over our heads, is it any wonder that God says things that go over our heads?

If you start whacking out parts of the Bible, or chuck the Bible altogether because there are things in it you cannot understand, you solve one problem: You don't have to explain the Trinity and other hard things. But for every problem you solve, you create a hundred more.

There are really only two errors you can fall into regarding the Trinity. You can emphasize oneness to the detriment of threeness, or you can emphasize threeness to the detriment of oneness. Both of these errors have been made for the last two thousand years.

The basic assertion of this doctrine is that the unity of the one God is complex. The three personal "subsistences" (as they are called) are coequal and coeternal centers of self-awareness, each being "I" in relation to two who are "you" and each partaking of the full divine essence (the "stuff" of deity, if we may dare to call it that) along with the other two. They are not three roles played by one person (that is modalism), nor are they three gods in a cluster (that is tritheism); the one God ("he") is also, and equally, "they" and "they" are always together and always cooperating, with the Father initiating, the Son complying, and the Spirit executing the will of both, which is his will also" (*Concise Theology*, 42).

Distortions of the Bible's Teaching About God

Two prominent ancient views about God deny the Trinity and were considered and then rejected by early Christians as false (as heresies).

1. Arianism, propounded by a Greek theologian named Arius in the 4th century A.D., holds that there is only one God, Jehovah, denying that Jesus and the Holy Spirit are God.
2. Sabellianism, propounded by Sabellius, also agrees that there is only one God, but maintains that He is only one person who appears in three different manifestations (Father, Son, Holy Spirit), like an actor changing costumes. It thus denies that Christ and the Holy Spirit are distinct persons within the one Being of God.

Arius, who lived in the early fourth century A.D. was a priest in North Africa who held the deity of the Father so highly that he denied that Jesus Christ and the Holy Spirit were also God, in every way equal to the Father. His was the first major ancient heresy regarding the doctrine of God. A modern heresy similar to it is unitarianism (The Unitarian Church), which likewise denies that Jesus Christ is God. Jehovah's Witnesses regard Arius as a forerunner of C. T. Russell, the founder of the sect. Arianism also has similarities with strict Mormonism, which claims that Jesus was created and not eternally divine.

Another heresy denies the eternal Trinity in favor of a God of one eternal person who merely shows Himself on different occasions as Father, Son, and Spirit. Sabellius, who lived around A.D. 250, was the first to champion this view called "modalism." Sabellius insisted that the one God appeared in three successive modes, first as Father, then as Son, and finally as the Holy Spirit. With the Arians, modalists maintain the unity of God; however, unlike the Arians, modalists also emphasize that Jesus Christ is fully God. Despite its commendable emphasis both on God's unity and on Jesus Christ's identity as God, modalism is flawed because it denies that the Father, the Son, and the Holy Spirit are distinct personally and eternally. Modalism tells us that God only appears in three different roles, leaving us unsure of who God really is behind or apart from these roles, or modes of manifestation. In contrast, the doctrine of the Trinity tells us that God is Father, Son, and Holy Spirit eternally.

The doctrine of the Trinity thus assures us that God's love toward us is nothing less than the same love that flows perfectly and eternally between the Father, the Son, and the Holy Spirit. But by denying these personal and eternal distinctions within the being of God, modalism (taught today by "oneness" Pentecostals) undermines our assurance of God's love for us and blurs the knowledge of God we enjoy through the clarity of the revealed doctrine of the Trinity.

Apart from these denials of the Trinity, one distortion of the Trinity remains a constant danger wherever the doctrine is not taught accurately. That danger is tritheism, a distortion of the Trinity that sees Father, Son, and Holy Spirit not as persons within the one Being of God, but instead as three distinct Gods. In this case, the threeness of God is not sufficiently integrated with His oneness. Tritheism is nowhere intentionally taught among Christians. Where it appears, it is the unfortunate result of inaccurate and careless teaching that allows any not to believe what the Bible from Genesis to Revelation consistently emphasizes: God is one.

In summary, then, we see that the doctrine of the Trinity is a vital doctrine. You cannot remain true to the teachings of the Scripture and hold to another position. You must whack something out of your Bible or add something to it. Consequently, we must give equal attention, value, and honor to each member of the Trinity. All non-Trinitarian teachings fall short of Scripture. They are fundamentally false and will distort not only a person's belief, but also his life if followed consistently.

All too often, we in the West with our smug self-assurance demand that God be understandable and reasonable. As spiritual "ugly Americans" we look down on God and insist that He conform to our expectations. But let me ask, how simple would the Bible have to be in order for everyone to understand everything about it? Should a person with an I.Q. of 150 be able to understand everything about it? How about a person with an I.Q. of 110? What about 85? Should a child of ten be able to understand it all? How about a child of two? Should everyone be able to understand everything about the Bible, or only some people? If some, then who? You yourself are able to understand things now that you were not able to understand ten years ago. It ought not to bother us if there are things we don't understand. I would be a little frightened if I understood everything about God. I would fear that He would be too simple to be able to solve all the problems. If I don't understand all the problems , why should I expect to understand all the solutions, or the solution giver? Let us decide to take God as He reveals Himself to us, and approach Him and His Word in humility and obedience.

We have finite minds. We will never be able to fully comprehend an infinite mind, or the Book that came out of it. The doctrine of the Trinity is a difficult doctrine; yet without committing intellectual suicide we can embrace it, realizing that the day will come when we shall know and understand more fully the God we worship. Sometimes, we have to see in order to believe. Other times, we must believe in order to see.

Speed Bump!

Slow down to be sure you've gotten the main points of this chapter.

Question
Answer

Q1. How many Gods does the Bible teach there are?

A1. The Bible teaches that there is only *one* God.

Q2. Who are Jesus and the Holy Spirit?

A2. In addition to God the Father, Jesus and the Holy Spirit are also called *God* in the Bible.

Q3. Can the doctrine of the Trinity be fully explained?

A3. Attempts to explain the doctrine of the Trinity fully fall short, as do all attempts to explain God fully. The statements of Scripture that form this doctrine must be taken by *faith* at face value.

Fill In the Blank

Question
Answer

Q1. How many Gods does the Bible teach there are?

A1. The Bible teaches that there is only _____ God.

Q2. Who are Jesus and the Holy Spirit?

A2. In addition to God the Father, Jesus and the Holy Spirit are also called _____ in the Bible.

Q3. Can the doctrine of the Trinity be fully explained?

A3. Attempts to explain the doctrine of the Trinity fully fall short, as do all attempts to explain God fully. The statements of Scripture that form this doctrine must be taken by _____ at face value.

For Discussion and Thought

1. Does it trouble you that the doctrine of the Trinity seems difficult to understand? Why or why not?

2. What would you tell a child who wanted to know about the Trinity?

3. Is it valid to accept the doctrine of the Trinity by faith, or do you think that is committing intellectual suicide?

4. What would it do to your confidence in the Bible to reject the Trinity because you could not understand it?

What If I Don't Believe?

There are two basic heresies regarding the Trinity, "modalism" and "tritheism."

1. Modalism contends that there is only one God, and that the Father, Jesus, and the Holy Spirit are merely separate manifestations of God. The personal distinctions Scripture records among Father, Son, and Holy Spirit are explained away as temporary or merely apparent, not real and not eternal. Thus modalism undercuts the great gospel truth that God loved us so much that the Father gave up His Son for us, thus assuring us that we can completely trust in His love.

2. Tritheism holds that there are three Gods, not one. No Christian consciously teaches tritheism, but it appears unwittingly wherever the doctrine of God's threeness-in-oneness is not taught accurately.

If you do not believe in the Trinity, you have fallen into one of these (or other) ancient heresies, which have been debated by church scholars for centuries. The complete biblical understanding is that God is one in substance but three in subsistence. Another way of putting it is that God is three and yet one, one and yet three. Certainly God does not want us to believe that 1+1+1=1, as if three $1 bills together total only $1. However, simple algebra shows us that the formula "three persons in one being" is not contrary to reason. Any beginning algebra student will recognize this equation as legitimate and solvable: $3x=1y$. But full understanding of the doctrine of the Trinity requires nothing less than full understanding of God. And that requires our being in heaven, at the least.

For Further Study

1. Scriptures.

- Deuteronomy 6:4
- Matthew 3:17–17
- Matthew 28:19
- 2 Corinthians 13:14
- 1 Peter 1:2

Read these passages and consider how they augment your understanding of the Trinity.

2. Books.

Several other books are very helpful for studying this subject further. They are listed below in general order of difficulty. If I could read only one of these, I would read the first one:

Know What You Believe, Paul Little
A Survey of Bible Doctrine, Charles Ryrie
Concise Theology, James I. Packer
Essential Truths of the Christian Faith, R. C. Sproul

5

Who Is God the Father?

Fathering is no easy task. I heard of one father who got a letter from his daughter in college. It read,

"Dear Dad,

I have decided to drop out of college. I'm failing everything anyway, and I have also come to realize that college is irrelevant. What does a degree mean, anyway? I mean, it's just a piece of paper! I have met a wonderful man, Gordo, who is a drummer in a rock and roll band. We are going to get married and live in a commune in Oregon. We'll let you know when we get settled. We'd love to have you and Mom come and visit us and gain greater cosmic consciousness.

Love, Susan.

P. S. Dear Dad. None of the above is true, but I did get a D in chemistry, and I do need $100.00."

Yes, fathering is a great challenge, and if done well, a rare art form. No rarer than being a good mother, but fathering is the subject of this chapter.

What makes a good father? If you were to close your eyes and envision the perfect father, what would you come up with? The answer would be different for different people, but one of the greatest fathers I have ever heard of was Casper ten Boom, the father of Corrie ten Boom. Corrie's family helped Jews escape from Nazi Germany during World War II. When Germany eventually occupied their homeland, the Netherlands, the ten Booms were discovered and imprisoned for aiding and abetting Jews. Their gripping story is told in the book, *The Hiding Place*, by Corrie ten Boom.

Corrie's father, Casper, was a watchmaker. But more than that, he was a kind, gentle, wise man who led his family with dignity, respect, and joy. Being a watchmaker, he was a man of precision, rising at the same time each day, appearing in the kitchen for breakfast at exactly the same time, and then stepping into his downstairs repair shop at exactly opening time. His schedule was a model of precision and efficiency.

Corrie writes of a special experience she had with her father when she was a little girl traveling with him on the train from their hometown to Amsterdam, to purchase watch parts for his repair shop:

Once—I must have been ten or eleven—I asked Father about a poem we had read at school the winter before. One line had described "a young man whose face was not shadowed by sexsin" [her spelling]. I had been far too shy to ask the teacher what it meant, and Mama had blushed scarlet when I consulted her. In those days just after the turn of the century sex was never discussed, even at home.

So the line had stuck in my head. "Sex," I was pretty sure, meant whether you were a boy or a girl, and "sin" made Tante (Aunt) Jans very angry, but what the two together meant I could not imagine. And so, seated next to Father in the train compartment, I suddenly asked, "Father, what is sexsin?"

He turned to look at me, as he always did when answering a question, but to my surprise he said nothing. At last he stood up, lifted his traveling case from the rack over our heads, and set it on the floor.

"Will you carry it off the train, Corrie?" he said. I stood up and tugged at it. It was crammed with the watches and spare parts he had purchased that morning. "It's too heavy," I said. "Yes," he said. "And it would be a pretty poor father who would ask his little girl to carry such a load. It's the same way, Corrie, with knowledge. Some knowledge is too heavy for children. When you are older and stronger you can bear it. For now you must trust me to carry it for you."

And I was satisfied. More than satisfied—wonderfully at peace. There were answers to this and all my hard questions—for now I was content to leave them in my father's keeping. I marveled at his on-the-spot wisdom (Excerpted from *The Hiding Place*, 30–31).

Later, as a teenager, Corrie also recalled a time when her father rose to superhuman status. She had fallen in love with a fine young man named Karel, and they had talked of marriage. His family objected, however, and he was forbidden to marry Corrie. His family chose a woman of position and wealth for him whom Karel had not loved but felt duty-bound to marry. When Corrie learned this it broke her heart.

How long I lay on my bed sobbing for the one love of my life, I do not know. Later, I heard Father's footsteps coming up the stairs. For a moment I was a little girl again waiting for him to tuck the blankets tight. But this was a hurt that no blanket could shut out, and suddenly I was afraid of what Father would say. Afraid he would say, "There'll be someone else soon," and that forever afterward this untruth would lie between us. For in some deep part of me I knew already that there would not—soon or ever—be anyone else.

The sweet cigar smell came into the room with Father, and of course he did not say the false, idle words.

"Corrie," he began instead, "do you know what hurts so very much? It's love. Love is the strongest force in the world, and when it is blocked that means pain.

"There are two things we can do when this happens. We can kill the love so that it stops hurting. But then of course part of us dies, too. Or, Corrie, we can ask God to open up another route for that love to travel.

"God loves Karel—even more than you do—and if you ask Him, He will give you His love for this man, a love nothing can prevent, nothing destroy. Whenever we cannot love in the old, human way, Corrie, God can give us the perfect way."

I did not know, as I listened to Father's footsteps winding back down the stairs, that he had given me more than the key to this hard moment. I did not know that he had put into my hands the secret that would open far darker rooms than this—places where there was not, on a human level, anything to love at all.

I was still in kindergarten in these matters of love. My task just then was to give up my feeling for Karel without giving up the joy and wonder that had grown with it. And so, that very hour, lying there on my bed, I whispered the enormous prayer:

"Lord, I give to You the way I feel about Karel, my thoughts about our future—oh, You know! Everything! Give me Your way of seeing Karel instead. Help me to love him that way. That much."

And even as I said the words I fell asleep (*The Hiding Place*, 47).

What a father! When I read about him, and ponder the wisdom of his words and deeds, I feel like a spiritual pygmy. I question if I walk on the same planet he did. It is hard for me to imagine a more complete father. When the Nazis arrested him for harboring Jews, he gladly went to his death rather than betray "God's chosen people."

His primary values were in the next world anyway. What he was doing in this life was to prepare for, and help others to prepare for, the next.

That is what an earthly father can be like. But earthly fathers, no matter how good, do not compare with our heavenly Father. In this chapter we will focus on the first person of the Trinity, God the Father, and understand His unique characteristics and roles as compared with God the Son and God the Holy Spirit.

Who Is God the Father?

The Father is God, the first member of the Trinity.

The Father of Us All, Including Jesus

God is a Spirit, but He is also our Father and all that that names implies. In Ephesians 1:2, we read, "Grace to you and peace from God our Father and the Lord Jesus Christ." In the next verse, we see that He is also the Father of Jesus: "Blessed be the God and Father of our Lord Jesus Christ."

Imagine in your mind's eye, as we did with Casper ten Boom, the finest earthly father you can imagine. God the Father is like that man, only more so. The Father is more lov- **The Father is** ing, more caring, more wise, more knowledge- **perfect love.** able, more zealous to provide for and protect, and more capable of fathering than any earthly father could be. We read in Hebrews 12:9–10 that

> We had earthly fathers to discipline us, and we respected them; shall we not much rather be subject to the Father of spirits and live? For they disciplined us for a short time as seemed best to them, but He disciplines us for our good, that we may share His holiness (NASB).

Earthly fathers discipline imperfectly, but God the Father perfectly. It is no accident that our heavenly Father chose to be called by the same word as our earthly fathers. In our day, some people have had bad fathers, and that is unfortunate. But some of us have had good fathers, and it helps us imagine what God the Father is like. Even those who have had bad fathers have seen and wished for good fathers, enough to have some concept of the goodness about God the Father.

In God the Father exists the perfection of the Godhead, so we know that He is loving, compassionate, just, holy, merciful, righteous, all-knowing, all-powerful, everywhere present, unchanging, and timeless.

The Head of the Trinity

As the Father, He is the head of the Trinity. First Corinthians 11:3 says, "Christ is the head of man, and the man is the head of a woman, and God is the head of Christ." In other words, the Father is the final authority in the Trinity. To understand this authority, we must understand the biblical idea of authority and submission. Ephesians 5:18 commands us to be filled with the Spirit. That command is followed by four participles. From the original Greek text, we understand that anytime a verb is followed by participles, the participles modify or define the verb. So the participles which follow the verb "to be filled" modify, or describe, the verb. The participles are, literally, "speaking," "melodying," "thanking," and "submitting." These are what you do if you are filled with the Spirit. The last participle, "submitting," is translated in the *New American Standard Bible*, "and be subject to one another in the fear of Christ." The submitting is a mutual submission, each person submitting to one another. It is the same "heart motive" as is found in Philippians 2:3–4, "Do nothing from selfishness or empty conceit, but with humility of mind let each of you regard one another as more important than himself; do not merely look out for your own personal interests, but also for the interests of others."

That is the spirit of mutual submission. However, while that is the spirit every Christian is to have toward others, there are, nevertheless, roles that Christians are to play toward others, even while having that spirit. For example, the instruction to "be subject to one another" in Ephesians 5 is followed by a description of three sets of relationships: husband/wife, parent/child, and master/slave. Paul describes how a husband is to submit to his wife and how his wife is to submit to her husband; how the parents are to submit to their children and how their children are to submit to their parents; how a master is to submit to his slave, and how the slave is to submit to his master.

Divine authority submits to the needs of those under authority.

The principle is laid down very clearly: In each relationship, the one in authority is to be submissive to the needs of the one under him, and the one under authority is to be submissive to the authority of the one over him. If this relationship exists, it results in peace, love and harmony.

Now the next question is, "Why did God give us those instructions?" I believe the answer is that He has created humanity to thrive under the same principles which operate within Trinity. The Father is the authority in the Trinity. Jesus is submissive to that authority. The Holy Spirit serves both the Father and the Son. Peace, love, and joy are the primary characteristics of that relationship. If we want peace, love, and joy, we must function the same way.

The key to all significant relationships is the servant heart. It is being subject to one another; caring for another more than you care for yourself; putting someone else first. When we don't do this, relationships wither and die. Thus, when it comes to the success of the significant relationships in our lives, mutual submission is the secret. Throughout the Bible, whenever authority is given to anyone, that authority is to be used for the good of the one under authority, whether it is government to citizens, elders to congregation, husbands to wives, parents to children, or masters to slaves. God gives no one authority to do mischief.

God the Father's authority extends then not only to the other members of the Trinity, but to us, and through the other members of the Trinity to us. God the Father is our Father. He has all authority over us, but He has already committed His word that His desire and intention is to do good to us forever (Ephesians 1:3–14). He is our Father. All His resources are at His disposal to "father" us.

Who is God the Father? He is the first person in the Trinity who is in authority in the Trinity and in all creation. He is our Heavenly Father, and, as our Father, is dedicated to doing good to us forever.

What Does God the Father Do?

God the Father initiates in His relationship within the Trinity, and He provides for and protects His children.

While all three members of the Trinity are equal in worth, they do not all have the same role. God the Father does things that the Son does not do. The Son does things that the Spirit does not do. Their roles are distinct, even while enjoying equality in a spirit of mutual submission. The distinct roles of the Father are related to His position as the One in authority in the Trinity.

In this chapter we learn that . . .

At least three things distinguish the life and ministry of God the Father from the Son and the Holy Spirit:

1. God the Father is Father of Jesus and of us all, and is the head of the Trinity.
2. God the Father is the architect and sovereign of all creation, original author of the plan of salvation, who exercises spiritual discipline over His children.
3. We worship God the Father in word and deed, highlighting His work in creation and sovereignty over it.

God the Father is the architect of all creation. What unfolds in history and happens in nature is the result of God the Father's purposes. God "works all things according to the counsel of His will" (Ephesians 1:11). He works our salvation out according to the "eternal purpose which He accomplished in Christ Jesus our Lord (Ephesians 3:11). The prophet Isaiah wrote, "The Lord of hosts has sworn saying, 'Surely, as I have thought so it shall come to pass, and as I have purposed so it shall stand. . . . This is the purpose that is purposed against the whole earth, and this is the hand that is stretched out over all the nations. For the Lord of hosts has purposed, and who will annul it? His hand is stretched out, and who will turn it back?' " (Isaiah 14:24, 26–27).

Yes, God has determined all that has happened, and all that will happen. This brings up several troubling questions. Did God create sin? The answer is "no." There is a difference between the directive will of God (those things He causes to happen), and His permissive will (those things He allows to happen). God does not desire that anyone should be eternally lost (1 Timothy 2:4). He has done everything in His power to prevent it, except override the capacity of man to choose. Yet we know that people will be eternally lost. God does not desire us to sin, but He allows us to sin. So, in saying that God has determined all that has happened and all that will happen is not to say that God created sin and is responsible for sin. But in His creation, He allowed for the possibility of sin.

The Father is creation's Architect.

God the Father was also active in the creation of the universe and world. However, so were the other members of the Trinity.

The Father Is the Author of the Plan of Salvation

God the Father established the process by which salvation would be accomplished. We see this explained clearly in Ephesians 1. God the Father determined the plan, which included our adoption as His spiritual children. Christ provided redemption for our sins through His death on the cross for us, forgave our sins, and gave us an inheritance. The Holy Spirit makes us secure in our inheritance, guarantees our salvation, and makes us eternally secure.

God the Father sent His Son into the world to redeem us. Jesus said in John 6:37–38, "All that the Father gives Me will come to Me, and the one who comes to Me I will by no means cast out. For I have come down from heaven, not to do My own will, but the will of Him who sent me."

The Father Exercises Spiritual Discipline

The Father is the disciplinarian of His children. We read in Hebrews 12:5–6, "My son, do not despise the chastening of the LORD, nor be discouraged when you are rebuked by Him; for whom the LORD loves He chastens, and scourges every son whom He receives."

All people are called the "offspring of God." In Acts 17:29, we read, "Being then the offspring of God, we ought not to think that the Divine Nature is like gold or silver or stone, an image formed by the art and thought of man." So, there is a sense in which God is the Father of all men as their Creator.

These, then, are some of the things which God the Father does that are different from the roles of God the Son and God the Holy Spirit.

The story is told of Joseph Kennedy, father of President John F. Kennedy, who once remarked of his granddaughter Caroline, Jack's daughter: "Caroline's very bright, smarter than you were, Jack, at that age."

"Yes, she is," agreed Jack. "But look who *she* has for a father."

And so it might be said of us, "Look who *we* have as a Father." No matter who our earthly father is, we have a heavenly Father who loves us, cares deeply about our welfare, and has committed His resources for our good.

How Do We Worship God the Father?

We worship God the Father in the sincerity of our heart, ascribing with words and deeds the worth due Him.

The Spirit of Worship

All three members of the Trinity deserve our worship. For example, Jesus said in John 4:23–24, speaking to the Samaritan woman at the well, "The hour is coming, and now is, when the true worshipers will worship the Father in spirit and truth; for the Father is seeking such to worship Him. God is spirit, and those who worship Him must worship in spirit and truth." While Jesus accepted the worship of others, He also encouraged worship of the Father.

Why Do I Need to Know About God the Father?

God the Father is not Jesus. Jesus is not God the Father. Neither is the Holy Spirit. God is three and yet one. That being the case, when we talk about God, sometimes we mean the triune God (all three in their triunity). But when we mean only the Father, we must understand His unique role, distinct from the other two members of the Trinity.

In addition, we see worship distinguished between the Father and the Son in Revelation 4 and 5. In chapter 4, we see worship of the Father in heaven:

"Behold, a throne was standing in heaven, and One sitting on the throne. And He who was sitting was like a jasper stone and a sardius in appearance; and there was a rainbow around the throne, like an emerald in appearance. . . . And from the throne proceed flashes of lightning and sounds and peals of thunder. And before the throne there was, as it were, a sea of glass like crystal. . . . The twenty-four elders will fall down before Him who sits on the throne, and will worship Him who lives forever and ever, and will cast their crowns before the throne, saying, "Worthy art Thou, our Lord and our God, to receive glory and honor and power; for Thou didst create all things, and because of Thy will they existed and were created"(Revelation 4:2, 3, 5, 6, 10, 11 NASB).

In this passage, we see God the Father worshipped as He sits in unimaginable majesty. Songs are sung to Him, praising Him for His creation. Yet in Chapter 5, we see the focus of worship turning to the Son:

Behold, the Lion that is from the tribe of Judah, the Root of David, has overcome so as to open the book and its seven seals. And I saw between the throne (with the four living creatures) and the elders a Lamb standing, as if slain. . . . And He came, and He took it out of the right hand of Him who sat on the throne. And when He had taken the book, the four living creatures and the twenty-four elders fell down before the Lamb, having each one a harp, and golden bowls full of incense, which are the prayers of the saints. And they sang a new song, saying, "Worthy art Thou to take the book, and to break its seals; for Thou wast slain, and didst purchase for God with Thy blood men from every tribe and tongue and people and nation.". . . I looked, and I heard the voice of many angels around the throne and the living creatures and the elders; and the number of them was myriads of myriads, and thousands of thousands, saying with a loud voice, "Worthy is the Lamb that was slain to receive power and riches and wisdom and might and honor and glory and blessing" (Revelation 5:5, 6, 7–9, 11–12 NASB).

In this passage, we see Jesus being praised in Son for giving his life to purchase the lives of those who believe in Him. Finally, we see them mentioned together:

And every created thing which is in heaven and on the earth and under the earth and on the sea, and all things in them, I heard saying, "To Him who sits on the throne, and to the Lamb, be blessing and honor and glory and dominion forever and ever" (Revelation 5:13 NASB).

While we do not want to make too great a distinction between worship of the Father and the worship of the Son, it is interesting that as you leaf through a hymnal, many of the hymns which focus on God the Father focus on His work in creation and His sovereignty over the earth, while the songs that focus on Jesus emphasize His work of salvation.

The Act of Worship

To worship God the Father is to publicly proclaim the worth due to Him. It is an activity to which all Christians are called and destined. In the Gospel of John (4:24), the Father seeks those who will worship Him in spirit and in truth. The apostle Peter wrote that we are to be a spiritual house, a holy priesthood, offering spiritual sacrifices acceptable to God through Jesus Christ (1 Peter 2:5). The Christian church was instructed to gather on the first day of the week for corporate worship. The most basic ingredients of worship in the early church were the reading and explanation of Scripture, prayer, the singing of hymns, and communion (the Lord's Supper). With the exception of the Lord's Supper, Jesus did not originate these Christian practices. They were carried over from the synagogue worship of the Jews.

As the church matured, worship services did not change much essentially. In modern America, the emphasis on the Lord's Supper has declined significantly, being observed in some churches quarterly or twice annually, and a much greater emphasis has been placed on singing and Bible teaching.

Since no instructions are given in the Bible as to what a worship service ought to look like, the Lord apparently intended flexibility. That flexibility should be used sensitively, so that the

The Father receives worship.

teachings of Scripture, the examples of worship in the Bible, the needs of the people, and the cultural circumstances in which a given church finds itself, will all combine to result in worship pleasing to the Lord and satisfying to those who worship.

We reflected in an earlier chapter that in a worship service the worshippers are the actors and God is the audience. We are there, not merely to get (instruction and inspiration), but also to give ourselves totally to God. Therefore, whatever the service, it should be such that it allows full participation of the worshippers. A service of purely passive spectators is not a worshipping congregation. While we talk about "activities" of worship, it must be emphasized that worship is a matter of the heart. Activities must facilitate the spirit of worship in the heart and activities of the sincere believer.

Speed Bump

Slow down to be sure you've gotten the main points of this chapter.

Question
Answer

Q1. Who is God the Father?

A1. The Father is God, the *first* member of the Trinity.

Q2. What does God the Father do?

A2. God the Father initiates in His *relationship* within the Trinity, and He provides for and protects His children.

Q3. How do we worship God the Father?

A3. We worship God the Father in the sincerity of our heart, ascribing with words and deeds the *worth* due Him.

Fill In the Blank

Question / Answer

Q1. Who is God the Father?

A1. The Father is God, the _____ member of the Trinity.

Q2. What does God the Father do?

A2. God the Father initiates in His _____ within the Trinity, and He provides for and protects His children.

Q3. How do we worship God the Father?

A3. We worship God the Father in the sincerity of our heart, ascribing with words and deeds the _____ due Him.

For Discussion and Thought

1. How does your experience with your earthly father help you in your relationship with your heavenly Father?

2. How does it hinder your relationship with your heavenly Father?

3. What specific areas do you think your concept of God the Father is limited by your experience with your earthly Father. How do you think you can help offset that experience?

4. Which comes first for you, meaningful heart attitude in worship or meaningful external activities? How do you think the two affect each other?

What If I Don't Believe?

1. I am out of step with this teaching of the Bible.

2. I am out of step with the consensus of church history.

3.   I am limited in my ability to attach the emotional value of good earthly fathers to God, thereby stunting my ability to develop a sense of emotional bonding with God. God intended earthly fathers to be a picture of Him as heavenly Father, and without that picture it is difficult to have an accurate and satisfying mental picture of God.

For Further Study

1. Scriptures.

- Matthew 3:17

- John 5:37

- Galatians 3:26

- Ephesians 1:3–6

- Hebrews 12:9

Read these passages and consider how they augment your understanding of God the Father.

2. Books.

There are several helpful books for studying this subject further. They are listed below in general order of difficulty. If I could only read one of them, I would read the first one:

Know What You Believe, Paul Little
A Survey of Bible Doctrine, Charles Ryrie
My God, Michael Green

If there were no God it would be necessary to invent Him.
■ **Voltaire**

6

Who Needs God?

In his book *Who Needs God?*, Rabbi Harold Kushner has written:

[In my ministry,] I deal with bright, successful people, people I genuinely like and admire, and I sense that something is missing in their lives. There is a lack of rootedness, a sense of having to figure things out by themselves because the past cannot be trusted as their guide. Their celebrations, from their children's birthday parties to a daughter's wedding to a business milestone, can be lots of fun but rarely soar to the level of joy. And as they grow older, I suspect they either confront or actively hide from confronting the thought that "there must be more to life that this."

There is spiritual vacuum at the center of their lives, and their lives betray this lack of an organizing vision, a sense of "this is who I am and what my life is fundamentally about." Some look for that center in their work, and are disappointed when corporations choose not to repay the loyalty they demanded or when retirement leaves them feeling useless. Some try to find it in their families, and don't understand why they are so hurt when adolescent children insist, "Let me lead my own life!" and adult children move to another state and call every other Sunday. There is a kind of nourishment our souls crave, even as our bodies need the right foods, sunshine, and exercise. Without that spiritual nourishment, our souls remain stunted and undeveloped (abridged from 9–11).

Who needs God? Every one of us. And we need God for many reasons. There *is* a kind of nourishment our souls need, just as our physical bodies do. Without it, our souls wither and die. St. Augustine, a fourth-century theologian from North Africa, and perhaps antiquity's greatest theologian, once wrote, "We were made for Thee, O God, and our souls are restless until they find their rest in Thee."

> *In this chapter we learn . . .*
>
> Three reasons why everyone needs God.
>
> 1. For hope in this life as well as hope for life after death.
> 2. To provide the absolute authority regarding truth and morals to guide individuals and society.
> 3. In order to have a sense of purpose and meaning in life.

What Hope Does God Give Us?

God gives us hope in the challenges of life in this world and hope for eternal life in the next.

Hope in This Life

We need God because we need hope in this life. When life overwhelms us, when circumstances and people push us beyond our capacity to cope, we need hope. These may be times of personal upheaval. Perhaps we are facing a health crisis. Perhaps we have just had a heart attack. Our life is hanging in the balance. The doctors don't know whether we are going to live or die. Instinctively, we turn to God. "Oh, God, help me!" we cry at our moment of great need. Or perhaps we learn that we have cancer, and our challenge isn't to stay alive for that moment, but to live for the next six months or six years with the sword of pain and death hanging always over our head. Instinctively, we turn to God.

Perhaps it is a financial calamity. Or perhaps it is not we who are in trouble but a loved one. A daughter is addicted to drugs, or a son's family is tearing apart. When airplanes go down, when floodwaters come up, when calamities hit, we instinctively turn to God. We long for hope, and at such times only God can give it.

Tragedy is a great clarifier. We see truly what is important and what is not. We get in touch with our mortality and our vulnerability, and see that we need God. No force in the universe can keep people from turning to Him then. And at such times, hope is beyond the capacity of man, but God will give it.

Hope for the Next Life

We also need God because we need hope for life after death. Toward the early part of the twentieth century it became fashionable to deny the existence of God and of the afterlife. We were brave. We had a fairly stable society, which Christianity had produced. We stood bravely on that stable society and denied the God who established it. Man is only a machine. Man is only an animal. We control our destiny. We will become greater and greater. We will become our own gods. Science, reason, and our intellect will continue to save us. That is all the salvation we need, we thought.

After more than a century of that world view we are recognizing the bankruptcy, the brazen foolishness, of that mind-set. Though we are advancing scientifically and technologically, we are regressing morally. We are destroying ourselves with greed, sexual immorality, and drugs. We are a nation in peril. We are realizing that we cannot control our own destiny in this life, let alone in the next.

People are no longer satisfied believing they are mere machines or animals. They are returning to the belief that they have souls and that there is life after death. They understand that no one has control over what happens after he dies. If anyone does control that, it would have to be God, and so people are turning to Him: *Oh, God, save us*, our hearts cry. *Make it safe for us to die.*

God gives hope for both lives—now and the next.

When I was a child I used to go swimming at a lake with a thirty-foot high-dive platform. I used to watch the other kids dive off of that and thought I could too. Some kids were afraid, but I wasn't. It looked simple. Exciting, even. When I climbed up the first time, I kept saying under my breath, "I'm not afraid. I'm not afraid." And I thought I wasn't.

But then I got to the top.

When I walked to the edge of the platform and looked down, thirty feet seemed like thirty miles. I was afraid. I nearly lost control of bodily functions. I couldn't go back, because there was a line of little lemmings on the ladder behind me, rushing to the sea, just as I was. It was one of life's most impossible moments. I couldn't go forward; I couldn't go backward. Worse, I couldn't remain where I was. Terrified, I put my mind in neutral and jumped. I nearly lost my stomach. I nearly lost my eyelids. I nearly lost my bathing suit. But I survived. On the ground before the climb it wasn't scary in the least. But up on the platform? Terrifying.

That is the way death is for those without Christ. When they are young and healthy, they aren't scared. But let them get old or sick. Get them up on the ladder with an accurate perspective, and they will be afraid. This fear is natural and God-given because it is not safe to die without God.

Why I need to know that people need God:

1. If I understand why people need God, I will see more clearly why *I* need God.
2. If I understand why people need God, I will be able to help other people see that He is the answer to their troubles and longings.
3. If I understand why people need God and why they turn to Him, I can experience peace and comfort in turmoil, hope in uncertainty, and a calmness when facing suffering or death.

It takes little insight into history, into society, into our own hearts, to realize that something is wrong with humankind. It is not that we cannot do good. Clearly, we can. But it is also that we cannot keep from doing evil. The Bible says that all have sinned and come short of the glory of God (Romans 3:23). It also says that the wages of this sin is death, or separation from God forever (Romans 6:23). Therefore, forgiveness of sin and reconciliation with God is our greatest need. This forgiveness, this reconciliation, is not a complicated affair. In John 3:16, we read, "For God so loved the world that He gave His only begotten Son, that whoever believes in Him should not perish but have eternal life." "To believe," in the biblical sense, does not mean mere intellectual assent, but a personal commitment to the object of that belief. To believe in God or His Son, therefore, means to accept who He is and place yourself under His jurisdiction, to follow Him. When you do, God will respond by giving you eternal life. This is discussed in great detail in volume two of this series, *Jesus: Knowing Our Savior*. God, then, gives hope of eternal life.

So, who needs God? We do. We need him for hope in this life and for the next.

What Moral Values Does God Give Us?

God gives us a secure basis for truth and falsehood, and for good and evil.

We need God in order to have a secure basis for truth and morality. Years ago when I led study tours to Israel and the Middle East I took people through the Holocaust Museum in Jerusalem. As you walk through it, there are artifacts on display from the concentration camps—barbed wire, instruments of torture, scientific equipment used in conducting human experiments on the Jews, and so on. There are also thousands of pictures depicting the incomprehensible inhumanity inflicted upon the Jewish people in those concentration camps. Skeletons with skin stretched tightly over them lean against barbed wire barricades, faces staring with hollow eyes.

If it would have been done to animals, it would have been an outrage. Because it was done to humans, it stands as one of the most horrible evils in the history of mankind. **Right and wrong** Holocaust: a word in the dictionary that no **cannot exist without** longer has to be explained. Everyone knows **God.** what it means. It is an event that everyone will agree was wrong. We may not agree whether abortion, capital punishment, or homosexuality are right or wrong. But we do agree that the Holocaust was wrong.

But was it wrong?

"Why was it wrong?" you cry. "Because you can't kill people just because you don't like them."

But I could say, "The Nazis passed laws sanctioning what they did. It was all within the law. They broke no laws. So why was it wrong if the majority of people thought that it was right?"

The problem is, if you cannot appeal to an authority higher than man, you cannot use the terms "right" and "wrong." You can say you don't like it, that it's cruel, that it shouldn't be done. But that is just your opinion. You cannot say it is wrong. Hitler thought it was right. You think it is wrong. Who is correct?

One person says it is wrong to kill, and another says it is right. Who says which one is correct?

One person says it is wrong to be sexually promiscuous, and another says it is right. Who says which one is correct?

One person says it is wrong to steal, and another says it is right. Who says which one is correct?

Terms like right and wrong can be used only if there is an unchanging obligatory moral base established by God. If you do not recognize God, there is no possibility of that moral base. It is as Dostoyevsky wrote in *The Brothers Karamazov*, "If there is no God, all things are permissible."

We also need God because His truth and morality form the

basis for social stability. If you do not have morals, if you do not have right and wrong, it eventually becomes difficult to have so-cial order because more and more people dis-agree about what makes for just laws. And so now in the United States, you cannot destroy habitat for the Golden Cheeked Warbler, a bird on the endangered species list, but you can abort a baby that is old enough to live outside the womb!

A shared view of right and wrong provides social stability.

Without a moral base, not only do you have difficulty agree-ing on morality for law and order, but you have trouble enforcing the laws you do have. There are laws against stealing, but businessmen on Wall Street steal with impunity, because they can get away with it. There are laws against bribes, graft, and kick-backs, but businesses and governments do it all the time. There are laws against drug abuse, driving while intoxicated, and pornography, and yet not enough citizens are willing to get in-volved to enforce these laws adequately. So social order begins to break down.

Who needs God? We do. There is no such thing as right and wrong without Him. There can be no social order without Him. Decent life in a decent country where the innocent are protected and opportunity is secure fades away. Morality must come from a higher level, or it will sink to the lowest levels. We need to get our truth from God and make it the basis of personal and social order.

The Ten Commandments give us a powerful and unchanging underpinning for personal and social order. Found in Exodus 20:1–17, they are these:

You shall have no other gods before Me.
You shall not make an idol for yourself.
You shall not take the name of the LORD your God in vain.
Remember the Sabbath day, to keep it holy.
Honor your father and your mother.
You shall not murder.
You shall not commit adultery.
You shall not steal.
You shall not bear false witness.
You shall not covet.

If this moral law were observed, most personal and social evils could be avoided. These powerful truths for personal and social order come from the lips of God. Who needs God? We all need God for personal and social order.

What Does God Give Us to Live For?

God satisfies the deepest longings of our souls.

There are many longings of the human soul, but two of the deepest are the longings for love and purpose. These are longings which God gave us, because He wants to be the One to fulfill them. In fact, He is the *only* One who can satisfy them fully.

However, most of us have trouble looking to God for the satisfaction of these longings and instead tend to look to people and things in this world. This is natural because even God uses people and things in this world to contribute the satisfaction of our longings. And, as long as things go well for us, this is a deceptively effective strategy. However, most of us cannot control people and things completely enough to be fully satisfied all the time. In fact, we are often unfulfilled much of the time.

Looking at the first longing for love, we find ourselves doing the very thing that destroys our love. We are obsessed with winning, with being number one, with getting life to go our way. Because of this drive to "succeed" we tend to see other people either as obstacles to our goals or as resources to be used in the pursuit of our goals. We either fight people or use them. As a result, many have lost the art of loving. Husbands do not know how to love their wives. Wives do not know how to love their husbands. Parents do not know how to love their children, and, therefore, children do not know how to love their parents. Co-workers, neighbors, relatives do not know how to love each other.

This breakdown in knowing how to love results in loneliness. We don't feel loved; therefore, we feel lonely. Today, even the "traditional" family is often no longer a unit, but a collection of individuals living under the same roof. Each one has his own bedroom, his own television and stereo, and each one has his own activity schedule. This is a certain recipe for loneliness. We seek more privacy and yet feel more alienated and lonely when we get it.

Only God can satisfy the deepest longing of our soul.

Looking at the second longing for purpose, we discover that

we are, again, doing the very thing that keeps us from having a sense of purpose. We were never created to live for ourselves. We were created to live for other people and for causes that are greater than ourselves. However, we spend our lives chasing material comfort and possessions. But there is no satisfying sense of purpose in selfish living. Therefore, to mask the sense of purposelessness and loneliness combined, we turn to work, alcohol, drugs, sex, sensual entertainment, Satanism and witchcraft, and to an alarming degree, we even commit suicide. Why? Because the things we live for don't satisfy.

The bumper sticker says, "The one who dies with the most toys wins." What a foolish philosophy! My guess is that the phrase was coined by someone under forty. He thinks he is running a race, but he will find out he is walking off a gangplank.

Though there are more people in the world than ever before, people are lonelier than ever before. And though we are a richer nation than ever before, never have more experienced such an acute lack of purpose.

Conclusion

God is our solution to our longing for love. He first loves us and by demonstration and then by teaching, through the Scriptures, shows us how to love others. 1 John 4:19 says, "We love God because He first loved us." That is the pattern for meaningful relationships. Others will love us as they perceive that we first love them. Whether it is in the family, the church, or society as a whole, others love us as they perceive our love for them. Selfishness, isolation, striving for success, being number one, all these militate against love. If we'll do it His way, God can help us love and feel loved while here on earth.

However, this world is not a perfect place. Our families may be dysfunctional, our friends unfaithful, our co-workers disloyal. Even when friends fail us in this life, we can turn to the Lord who loves us without limit and without end. He values us if no one else does. We can receive emotional support from God Himself to help us grieve through the pain of lost love in this life. And beyond that, we can look forward to eternity when God will love us and we will love God face to face. At the same time, we will be surrounded in heaven by God's children of all ages who will also love us perfectly. We will belong to a great spiritual family and never feel lonely again.

In addition, God is our solution to our longing for purpose. As we turn from living for ourselves to living for others and living for the advancement of heaven's influence on earth, we begin to have a deep sense of purpose. President John Kennedy once said, "Ask not what your country can do for you. Ask what you can do for your country." In principle, God asks the same of us. We ask, not what others can do for us, but what we can do for others. In that pursuit, we find a sense of purpose in this life.

Not only does God give us a sense of purpose in this life, but He also holds out to us a sense of purpose throughout eternity. We will rule and reign with Him in heaven forever. We will be gifted for great service to and with Him. We will accomplish more good in eternity than our minds have the ability to imagine.

In Matthew 22:37–39, Jesus said, " 'You shall love the LORD your God with all your heart, with all your soul, and with all your mind.' This is the great and foremost commandment. And a second is like it, 'You shall love your neighbor as yourself.' " These commandments are the keys to meeting our deepest longings for love and purpose.

God is the ultimate answer for the deep longings of our soul, both in this life and in the life to come. Who needs God? We do . . . for love and for purpose, to fulfill the deepest longings of our soul.

In his book *The Man in the Mirror*, Patrick Morley writes of a prominent Florida attorney:

> "My life has no meaning—no purpose," he [said]. "It's as though I've been chasing the wind all these years."
>
> As Tom unfolded the story of his life, the vast array of accomplishments on his résumé awed me. A man of stature, his list of credits revealed a Who's Who in the legal field. I would have imagined him to be a satisfied man, were it not for the stream of tears that diluted the value of those achievements.
>
> Tom had reached the pinnacle of professional success, yet still ached for a sense of purpose in his life.
>
> "Maybe God will have some answers," he thought.
>
> What interested Tom most was the peace he saw in some of the men involved with the prayer breakfast. Over the six months

that followed, he was surprised to learn these men attributed their sense of peace and purpose to a "personal" relationship with God through Jesus Christ.

"I've always attended church," he insisted.

"We're not talking about attending church, although that's important. What we're talking about, Tom, is a relationship with the living, personal God.

"We are not talking about working your way into God's favor, but acknowledging it's impossible to work your way in. The only way into God's favor is to receive the free gift of eternal life that comes by trusting Christ with your life."

"Well, I've been a faithful churchman for over thirty years. Are you trying to tell me I've wasted all those years? I just can't believe you would even suggest such a thing!"

I replied, "Tom, if church has been such an important part of your life, why are we together today talking about your feelings of emptiness and lack of purpose?"

Tom is not alone. He lived the first fifty-eight years of his life without giving much attention to why he thought, said, and did things. Many people are like Tom. Just going through the motions.

You don't have to be like Tom. A sense of love and being loved can be yours. You can gain that sense from God Himself and from people whose lives are fully devoted to Him. You can have a sense of purpose, in the same way, by devoting yourself to His causes.

It is as C.S. Lewis, a British Christian scholar who died in 1964, once wrote, speaking of the relationship between living for this world and living for the next world: "Shoot for the heaven, and you get earth thrown in. Shoot for earth and you get neither."

Who needs God? We all do.

Speed Bump!

Slow down to be sure you've gotten the main points of this chapter.

Question
Answer

Q1. What hope does God give us?

A1. God gives us hope in the *challenges* of life in this world and hope for *eternal* life in the next.

Q2. What moral values does God give us?

A2. God gives us a *secure* basis for truth and falsehood, and for good and evil.

Q3. What does God give us to live for?

A3. God satisfies the deepest *longings* of our souls.

Fill In the Blank

Question
Answer

Q1. What hope does God give us?

A1. God gives us hope in the _____ of life in this world and hope for _____ life in the next.

Q2. What moral values does God give us?

A2. God gives us a _____ basis for truth and falsehood, and for good and evil.

Q3. What does God give us to live for?

A3. God satisfies the deepest _____ of our souls.

For Discussion and Thought

1. What evidence do you see in American culture that there is a God-shaped vacuum in every human heart?

2. Why do people not admit to feeling their need for God?

3. What do people use in the absence of God to give them hope in this life and for the next?

4. What do people use in the absence of absolute moral values to order their own lives or society?

5. What do people use in the absence of God for purpose and meaning?

6. What do you think could be done to help a person see or feel a need for God?

What If I Don't Believe?

Personal Consequences.

1. You are forced to try to find hope in a world that offers no hope. If the past is meaningless (chance evolution) and the future is meaningless (absolute annihilation), then you cannot escape living in a meaningless present.

2. You are forced to find values to live by when, in fact, all truth is relative. You must try to find a way of getting society to agree on what is right and wrong, even though there is no basis for the agreement. You are forced to deal with the guilt when you do things you believe to be wrong, but you have no external reason to believe they are wrong.

3. You are forced to try to find purpose and meaning, even though life is absurd and meaningless without God. You must try to find meaning in work, in relationships, in success, in entertainment, in drugs or alcohol, or some other way. You must find temporary meaning in the absence of ultimate meaning.

4. If you cannot find hope, values, purpose, and meaning, you must find things to occupy your mind so that you don't have to think about it. This may help to explain American preoccupation with entertainment and the media. If the radio, stereo, and television are always on, you never have to think. You never have to admit to the hopelessness of your situation.

Societal Consequences.
The social consequences are merely the personal consequences multiplied by everyone else.

1. Society does not offer its younger generation hope. Therefore, the new generation has to experiment with bizarre and unusual options. There is no hope in the old options, so experimentation with new options offers hope. That helps to explain why the younger generation is preoccupied with things that numb the meaninglessness. Music, sex, television, video games, alcohol, and drugs offer temporary pleasure in the absence of permanent hope. This is also why some young people commit suicide. They lose hope that there will ever be any hope.

2. Law and order breaks down. People are not willing to follow the rules that exist for the sake of the masses or for the protection of the innocent.

They will do whatever they can get away with if it gives them temporary pleasure or meaning.

3. We become a nation of workaholics because we derive our meaning solely from work.

4. The family begins to break down because family members are out for themselves.

5. Society overall begins to deteriorate because the values of hard work, sacrifice, looking out for the other guy, honesty, integrity, chastity, and patriotism are replaced with selfishness, the pursuit of pleasure, and evading laws.

For Further Study

1. Scripture Passages.
Several passages in the Bible speak of humanity's need for God.

- Proverbs 1:20–33

- Acts 17:16–34

- Romans 1:18–2:2

- 1 Corinthians 15:12–19

- Galatians 5:19–23

If you wish to study further, read these passages and consider how they contribute to your understanding of our need for God.

2. Books.
There are helpful books for studying this subject further. They are listed below in general order of difficulty. If I could only read one of these, I would read the first one:

Hope for the Troubled Heart, Billy Graham
Tramp for the Lord, Corrie ten Boom
Who Needs God? Harold Kushner (Jewish rabbi. You will not agree with all of his conclusions. Read with discretion.)
Knowing God, J. I. Packer

God is like a person who clears His throat
while hiding and so gives himself away.
■ **Meister Eckhardt**

7

How Can We Know God?

When I was in college, I introduced my best friend to a girl whom he eventually married. That was twenty-five years ago, and they still have a great marriage. Let me tell you how it happened.

I was attending a small Christian liberal arts college, and my class had a pre-school party the weekend before my third year began, and my friend, Joe Barclay (not his real name) went with me. He was interested in having me get him a date, and he wanted to look over the possibilities at the party. It was an outdoor barbecue, and shortly after we got there, Joe's radar zeroed in on a tall, attractive California girl. We called her (affectionately) "The Amazon." She had a deep bronze summer tan, long, straight brown hair, a classic profile, and a gentle smile.

If Joe had been a smoke detector, he would have started beeping! "What's her name?" he asked with a thinly disguised intensity.

"Meredith McCall," (not *her* real name, either) I replied.

"Do you know her?"

"Yes."

"Can you get me a date with her?"

"I bet I can," I replied, wondering if I really could.

A week later I saw Meredith and plucked up my courage.

"Meredith, a good friend of mine would like to have a date with you. You've never met him, but I think you would really like him. He's a good-looking guy, a tremendous athlete, and a committed Christian." I said more than that. Much more than that. I felt responsible for the success of this endeavor. A vast sense of failure welled up within me at the prospect that she might not go along with it. My mouth was dry. My palms were sweating. I begin to gabble. I tried to make Joe sound as good as I could without lying. I might have lied a little. After about a two minute non-stop barrage of words, I came up for breath. Meredith was smiling. She said, "All right Max. If you recommend him that highly, I'd be happy to go out with him."

Bingo! I hadn't failed. Joe would have his date with the Amazon.

We double-dated on their first date, and I felt as though the two of them combined to form a "relationship rocket." I had merely lit the fuse. Off they went into the heavens together. Around Thanksgiving Joe told me that he and Meredith were getting married. I was floored, but happy for them. They were from solid Christian homes, had excellent modeling from their parents, and were both living for the Lord. Normally, I am pretty nervous about "sudden" engagements, but not this one. Both sets of parents were supportive, and it seemed right from the beginning. Seven months later, I flew to California to be best man at a lovely summer wedding, with the kind of weather we will be having in heaven!

From there, their relationship has grown to be a model of selfless love to each other and to their children. Of course, they don't think so, but that's part of their success. They don't feel that they have "arrived." Their marriage is not perfect, because neither of them is perfect. All I know is that the world and the church would be a whole lot better off if there were more marriages like theirs.

As I think about their relationship, there was a clear progression. Joe learned about Meredith, moved toward her, and established a relationship. That culminated in marriage, after which they adjusted themselves to each other, growing in understanding and appreciation and a desire to please and accommodate each other. Finally, as they weathered trials together, the pain and suffering brought them closer together, and through it they forged a relationship of depth and maturity which could never have been realized without the refining fire.

In this chapter we learn . . .

Three ways by which we know God:

1. We learn about God through the Bible, through nature, and through our conscience.
2. We meet God by saying "yes" to God's invitation to come to Him.
3. We grow in our relationship with God when we learn of God's character and commands, and then trust and obey Him.

I have taken some time to describe their relationship because it is comparable to how our relationship with God begins and deepens. It also helps us take some of the mystery out of our relationship with

Him, and it shows how we can understand more completely how to know Him.

How Can We Learn About God?

We learn about God through the Bible, through nature, and through our conscience.

Joe's first step was to get to know Meredith. I had told him what I knew about her, and he had observed her from afar, but then he needed to learn about her. So, too, we can learn about God.

God has given us three primary ways to know about Him. First, through the Bible. Even atheists can learn about the God they don't believe in by reading the Bible. They can know that if

We learn about God through the Bible.

this God did exist, this is what He would be like. Most of us learn about God initially from well-known Bible stories. Moses and the Exodus, David and Goliath, Daniel in the lions' den, Jesus' miracles or parables, the Crucifixion and the Resurrection, and so on. Even if you watch the television quiz show "Jeopardy!" you will see questions about these stories. And as we learn more about the Bible, we will discover about more of God's power, intelligence, presence, love, justice, compassion, even his wrath. We learn about God from the Bible.

A second source for learning about God is "nature." In the Bible we read that "what may be known of God is manifest . . . for God has shown it to them. . . . For since the creation of the world His invisible attributes—his eternal power and Godhead— are clearly seen, being understood by the things that are made" (Romans 1:19–20).

Unless this impulse is squashed, when one looks into the starry heavens on an exceptionally clear night, the jaw goes slack, the eyes widen, and the irrepressible thought pops to the surface

We learn about God through nature.

of the mind, "There must be a God." Abraham Lincoln once said, "I can see how it might be possible for a man to look down upon the earth and be an atheist, but I cannot conceive how he could look up into the heavens and say there is no God." We see that He is a God of stupendous power and magnitude. So, too, when we gape for the first time at the Grand Canyon, or Yosemite Valley, or

Rocky Mountain National Park. We see that God is a God of knee-weakening beauty, of astonishing creativity, of endless variety, and, somehow, of goodness. We learn about God from nature.

A third avenue for learning about God is through our conscience plus reflection. The Bible tells us that God put eternity into the heart of man (Ecclesiastes 3:11). That is, He has created man with a capacity to look for, long for, understand, and embrace the divine. **We learn about God through conscience.** When one reflects on truth with this innate knack for the eternal, one can learn about God.

The question is, "What do you do with this information?" You will either move toward God or away from Him. You may try to stand still, only you aren't standing. You're floating downstream away from Him, you just don't realize it. Joe moved toward Meredith. If he hadn't, they never would have met. They never would have married. So it is with God. If you move toward Him, you can meet Him. If you move away from Him, or (from your viewpoint) stand still, you will not meet Him.

How Do We Meet God?

We meet God by saying "yes" to God's invitation to come to Him.

I don't know how Joe asked Meredith to marry him. But the day came when he must have said something like, "Meredith, I love you. Over the past months, you have learned a lot about me. We have talked a lot, and I have told you everything I know that might be relevant to you in assessing my worthiness as a husband. We have spent a lot of time together, and you have had an opportunity to observe my personality and character. I have done the same with you. Based on what you know of me, will you marry me?"

Meredith also knew the implications of that question. She knew about the biblical roles of husband and wife. She understood Joe's chosen profession, the ministry, and that she would probably never be rich or famous. She would be a "pastor's wife." There was a good deal to give up, she knew, but also a good deal to be gained. She understood that satisfying relationships are what makes life worth living, and that Joe possessed such qualities that, she believed, he could offer her a deeply satisfying relationship until death separated them. Assessing the pros and cons, Meredith said, "Yes."

Something similar happens between us and God. God says that He loves us (John 3:16). He reveals a lot of other information about Himself in the Scripture, nature, and through our conscience. "Will you be my child?" he asks.

This is more remarkable than any marriage proposal because God is so far above us. Nevertheless, will we accept His offer? Like the courted lover, we have the power to say "no." But if we say "yes," we are united with Him forever.

It is unlike the human relationship, however, in that, when a woman refuses a marriage proposal, she may find someone else. Nothing bad will necessarily happen to her if she rejects him. Something even better might happen. However, rejecting God is the gravest of all human acts. To be separated from God forever is unthinkable to those who understand the implications.

Why Do I Need To Know God?

1. If I do not know God, my soul is lost forever.
2. If I do not know God, I have no ultimate answers for my deepest questions and longings.
3. If I do not know God, I have no lasting truth, guidance, and comfort in life's trials.
4. If I do not know God, I have no biblical answers to give to others in their difficulties and questionings.

But, back to the question, "How can we meet God?" First, we must understand He asks us to come to Him. "Behold, I stand at the door and knock; If anyone hears My voice and opens the door, I will come in to him and dine with him, and he with Me" (Revelation 3:20). This invitation of fellowship with God reveals His desire for a close relationship with us.

We meet God by saying yes to Him. Then, we must say "yes" to the invitation to enter into a relationship with Him. If we do, it means that we are no longer masters of our own lives.

Maybe you are familiar with the poem "Invictus":

> Out of the night that covers me,
> Black as the Pit from pole to pole,

I thank whatever gods may be
For my unconquerable soul.

In the fell clutch of circumstance,
I have not winced nor cried aloud;
Under the bludgeonings of chance
My head is bloody, but unbowed.

It matters not how straight the gate,
How charged with punishment the scroll.
I am the master of my fate;
I am the captain of my soul.

■ **William Ernest Hensley**

When I first read that poem, as a new Christian, it stirred me in a way that is difficult to put into words. I longed to have control over my life and had the momentary illusion that I could. But soon I began to see that the words were sheer idiocy. It seemed like a man who stands before a benevolent king, being offered half the kingdom in return for homage, and the man says, "Forget it, I am the master of my fate, I am the captain of my soul," and promptly throws himself into the mouth of a volcano. So you are the master of your fate, captain of your soul! What virtue is there in being captain of your soul if it results in your destruction?

God beckons us, like a suitor, to His love. We answer "yes" or "no." If "yes," our new relationship entails certain changes. We are no longer our own masters. We must adjust ourselves to the requirements of Him who is Lord. We cannot say "yes" to God and "no" to all He stands for, any more than Meredith could say "yes" to Joe, and then still see other men, refuse to keep house with him, and refuse to bear or care for their children. When we say "yes" to God, we say "yes" to all we understand of His expectations for us.

It may be that, after having said "yes," we learn about an expectation He had for us that we did not understand in the beginning. That often throws Christians into crisis. The most common one is that God does not eliminate the suffering of Christians. But that expectation and disappointment is worked through with God's help, just as things unforeseen in a marriage are worked through after the ceremony.

How do we meet God? We say "yes" to His invitation, and give ourselves to Him. It is the starting point for knowing God.

How Can We Grow In Our Relationship With God?

We grow in our relationship with God when we learn of God's character and commands, and then trust and obey Him.

Growing in our relationship with God involves learning what He asks of us and doing our best to accomplish it. Specifically, learning involves reading the Bible with an attitude of compliance, looking to see how our lives might not match what is taught, and then striving to align ourselves with the truth.

First Peter 2:2 says we should be as newborn babes who "desire the milk of the word," that we might grow in respect to salvation. As we give serious attention to heeding the Scripture, we will grow and mature as Christians. Romans 6:17 reads, "But God be thanked that though you were slaves of sin, yet you obeyed from the heart that form of doctrine to which you were delivered." The Roman Christians were not obedient with gritted teeth or clenched fists. They were obedient from the heart, which is what God asks of us.

We grow in our relationship with God by obeying Him.

In his marvelous book *Knowing God*, J.I. Packer lists four activities through which we know God:

1. Listening to God's Word and receiving it as the Holy Spirit interprets it in application to oneself.
2. Noting God's nature and character, as His Word and works reveal it.
3. Accepting His invitations, and doing what He commands.
4. Recognizing, and rejoicing in, the love that He has shown in drawing one into this divine fellowship. (32).

We might say this means:

1. Honoring God's Word.
2. Trusting God's character.
3. Obeying Him.
4. Enjoying Him.

We have already looked at honoring God's Word, so let's now look at why trusting God's character is essential for growth. If we are to grow, we must trust God, especially when that means obeying Him in the difficult things.

I enjoy some of the old black-and-white movies based on classic literature. In the 1940 version of *The Mark of Zorro*, Tyrone Power plays the "Robin Hood of California" in a fairly faithful production of the original book. In the movie, there is a remarkable "chase" scene in which Zorro is fleeing in the dead of night from a band of Spanish army officers. He is dressed in black, and his horse, of course, is jet black. Racing at breakneck speed through woods, over creeks, along narrow paths, Zorro is finally cornered on a bridge suspended about twenty feet over a river. In one of the most remarkable stunts I have ever seen in a movie, the rider (probably not Tyrone Power) turned the horse toward the railing on the bridge, which was about four-and-a-half feet high, and spurred him. The horse jumped over the railing, into the river below, with the rider still on him. It swam downstream in a hail of bullets from the bridge, and once again, Zorro made a cunning escape.

My question is, how in the world did that stunt rider get that horse to jump over that railing into the black abyss below? That is one of the most unnatural things a horse would ever do. A horse would be almost as likely to dance ballet or swim a backstroke as to jump into a black abyss.

I learned the answer from those who train horses. The secret is that the rider must never ask the horse to do anything that hurts it. The rider first gets the horse to do little stunts that seem dangerous, but the horse does not get hurt. So the trainer graduates to stunts of medium difficulty and danger. Finally, he graduates to major stunts. After years of training, the horse learns to trust the rider, because nothing traumatizing has ever happened to him in the past. As a result, he will do almost anything the rider asks of him in the future. Obviously, this rider had spent a lot of time working with that horse, and a high degree of trust had developed. The horse never hesitated. Over the rail and into the river. If you know anything about horses, it will almost bring tears to your eyes to imagine the amount of work and trust that had to have gone into such a bold move.

That is where God wants to get us. He wants to get us to the point at which we will go off a cliff for Him if we understand that He is the one who is asking. The only way we will ever do that is if we learn to deeply trust His character.

Trust leads us to "accepting His invitations and doing what He commands." Jesus said, "Come to Me, all you who labor and are heavy laden, and I will give you rest. Take My yoke upon you and learn from Me, for I am gentle and lowly in heart, and you will find rest for your souls. For My yoke is easy, and My burden is light" (Matthew 11:28–30). What an invitation! How we would grow if we were to accept it. I have found that whenever life's load is getting too heavy for me to bear, I am trying to carry something Jesus never intended for me to carry. I am taking up a yoke which only He can bear. When I lay that yoke down, life gets bearable again. Let me explain.

We grow in our relationship with God by trusting Him.

A little over a year before the writing of this book, I came down with a serious illness. I had to leave the church I was pastoring because I had become disabled and, more than a year later, I was still unable to pastor. It was easy to become worried about the future. *Who's going to pay the bills? Would I ever be well enough to function normally again? Is the rest of the world going to forget about me? Will I ever be able to pastor a church again? Will I be in dreadful physical pain the rest of my life? Would I ever be able to live as I had before?*

The evil one took these matchboxes of worry, struck them, and fanned them into an inferno of insecurity and anxiety. Time and time again, I would read Matthew 6:27–34:

> Which of you by worrying can add one cubit to his stature? So why do you worry about clothing? Consider the lilies of the field how they grow: they neither toil nor spin; and yet I say to you that even Solomon in all his glory was not arrayed like one of these. Now if God so clothes the grass of the field, which today is, and tomorrow is thrown into the oven, will He not much more clothe you, O you of little faith? Therefore do not worry, saying, 'What shall we eat?' or 'What shall we drink?' or 'What shall we wear?' For after all these things the Gentiles seek. For your heavenly Father knows that you need all these things. But seek first the kingdom of God and His righteousness, and all these things shall be added to you. Therefore do not worry about tomorrow, for tomorrow will worry about its own things. Sufficient for the day is its own trouble.

When I would read this passage, I knew that I was carrying a burden which Jesus never intended me to carry. If I would come to Him, and lay the burden down, I could find rest for my soul. It wasn't easy, and I didn't execute it perfectly, but at least I understood that if I could bring myself to trust God, I could stop worrying. That is what Packer means by accepting God's invitations.

"Doing what He commands" is tied closely to accepting His invitations. We obey God when we believe what He says. We don't obey when we don't believe. If we fully believed that God commands only what is for our benefit and prohibits only what would harm us, we would never flagrantly disobey Him. Because of our creaturely weakness, in the face of temptation we have not caused, we might trip up and fall, but we would not disobey Him with malice and forethought.

Trusting and obeying God opens the door to the delights of "recognizing and rejoicing in the love He has shown in drawing us into His divine fellowship." This opportunity may be hard for us to appreciate if we do not grasp the significance of what God has done. The poet Carl Sandburg once said, "Without great audiences, there can be no great poets." An audience must have the capacity to recognize greatness before a great poet will ever get the recognition he deserves. So true. In the analogy, God is the Great Poet and we are the audience. If we do not recognize the greatness of the Poet, He will not get the recognition from us that He deserves. However, as we grow in our capacity to recognize and appreciate His greatness, we learn to rejoice in what God has done for us. We learn to enjoy God. Even in the firestorms of life, we can smile with joy as we enjoy God.

We grow in God by enjoying Him.

Conclusion

In this world we cannot know God in exactly the same way we know a human being. Another human being looks into our eyes as we speak and talks to us in return. We get clear and immediate answers to our questions. Body language, facial expressions, and vocal inflections tell us what the other person is thinking and feeling. The level of communication allows us to have a degree of emotional intimacy that is often not possible with God. Having a relationship with God is like relating to a person whose face you cannot see, who does not talk with you aloud, and in whose voice you cannot read humor or sadness. On the other hand, we can know God, and He does communicate to us. There is a spiritual intimacy we can have with Him that we cannot have with another person, because God has answers that people do not have, and God gives comfort and hope that people cannot give.

When I was terribly sick and in dreadful pain, it was God to whom I turned. My dear wife, Margie, was a source of God's grace for which I shall be eternally grateful, but even she could not do what God did for me. I turned to Him again and again, often in tears, pleading with God to take away the pain. I read and read the Psalms and saw that David was not shy about telling God how he hurt. He even pleaded with God to take away the pain. If David could do it, so could I. I also read the Crucifixion account over and over. Jesus suffered so much for me, and I had no capacity to grasp just how much until I had had a good taste of suffering myself. I clung to the promise that His grace would be sufficient for me (2 Corinthians 12:9). Often, I did not feel that it was. But as I look back, it must have been because here I am.

I also contemplated the throne room chapters in Revelation 4 and 5. I took consolation in the hope of one day being there and singing His praises without pain.

The holiness of God also became a vivid concept to me, and a terribly important one. Somehow my pain helped me understand and appreciate His holiness more than ever. Night was always the worst time. There were many evenings when I thought I just couldn't stand to go through another night. And yet the nights came, and I was still alive, so what option was there but to go through them? In whispers I would quote the great "holiness" chapter of the Bible, Isaiah 6:1–8. When I finished that, I would softly sing the hymn, "Holy, Holy, Holy, Lord God Almighty! Early in the morning our song shall rise to Thee; Holy, holy, holy! merciful and mighty! God in three persons, blessed Trinity." After I had sung all four stanzas I would start over with Isaiah 6. When I had finished Isaiah 6, I would sing "Holy, Holy, Holy" again, until I finally fell asleep.

Somehow, in the middle of the pain and the distress, God was there. I did not "feel" His presence, but I was comforted by Him in a way that no human could have comforted me.

So, we cannot know God in exactly the same way we know other human beings, but we can know God in a way that we cannot know other human beings. We must never demand to know God in exactly the same way that we know other people. We must seek God, and we can know Him, in a way that we cannot know other people. We know Him by learning about Him, by approaching Him in faith, by seeking to align our lives with whatever we understand He requires of us, and by clinging to Him in the difficult times.

Speed Bump!

Slow down to be sure you've gotten the main points of this chapter.

Question Answer

Q1. How can we learn about God?

A1. We learn about God through the *Bible*, through *nature*, and through our *conscience*.

Q2. How can we meet God?

A2. We meet God by saying *"yes"* to God's invitation to come to Him.

Q3. How can we grow in our relationship with God?

A3. We grow in our relationship with God when we learn of God's character and commands, and then *trust* and *obey* Him.

Fill In the Blank

Question Answer

Q1. How can we learn about God?

A1. We learn about God through the _____, through _____, and through our _____.

Q2. How can we meet God?

A2. We meet God by saying "_____" to God's invitation to come to Him.

Q3. How can we grow in our relationship with God?

A3. We grow in our relationship with God when we learn of God's character and commands, and then _____ and _____ Him.

For Discussion and Thought

1. The apostle Paul wrote in Philippians 3:7–10, "But whatever things were gain to me, those things I have counted as loss for the sake of Christ.

More than that, I count all things to be loss in view of the surpassing value of knowing Christ Jesus my Lord, for whom I have *suffered the loss of all things*, and count them but rubbish in order that I may gain Christ, and may be found in Him, not having a righteousness of my own derived from the Law, but that which is through faith in Christ, the righteousness which comes from God on the basis of faith, that I may know Him, and the power of His resurrection and the fellowship of His *sufferings*" (italics mine, NASB).

Because there is a link between suffering and knowing God, how do you think suffering might help you to know God? (See additional Scripture passages on suffering under "For Further Study.")

2. What are some of the ways that knowing God is like knowing a human being, and what are some ways that it is not?

3. How are some of the specific things you do to get to know God the same as things you do to get to know humans? How are they different?

4. Do you think you will ever know God as well as you would like to? Why or why not?

5. How do you deal with the fact that you may not know God as well as you would like to or think you ought to? What role do you think that faith and patience might play in being content in your relationship with God?

What If I Don't Believe?

1. If I don't believe that I can know God, then I would have no reason to make a move toward Him. I would have to consider the biblical offers to know Him as false.

2. I would have no hope of ever having life's essential questions answered or its essential problems solved.

3. If I don't believe that I can know God, it might be because I don't believe that there is a God. But if, on the other hand, I believed there was a God but could not know Him, it seems likely to cause despair and hopelessness.

For Further Study

1. Scriptures.
A number of important passages address the subject of knowing God:

- John 17:13
- Acts 22:14
- 1 Corinthians 1:21
- 1 Corinthians 2:9–16
- Galatians 4:8–9
- Ephesians 3:14–19
- 1 John 4:6–8
- 1 John 5:2
- 1 John 5:20

  Passages dealing with suffering include:

- Philippians 4:10
- James 1:2–5
- 1 Peter 2:19–24
- 1 Peter 3:8–9

  Read these passages for additional information on knowing God.

2. Books.
There are several helpful books for studying this subject further. They are listed below in general order of difficulty. If I could only read one of these, I would read the first one:

My God, Michael Green
Loving God, Charles Colson
Rediscovering Holiness, James I. Packer
Knowing God, James I. Packer
Disappointment With God, Philip Yancey

8

How Do We Pursue God?

Have you ever wondered why you do not have a stronger appetite for God? Have you ever wondered why, when your mind tells you that He is the most important thing in your life, your will and your emotions think you're lying? Have you ever wondered why, when you pit God against television, work, tennis or sleep, God always loses? Have you ever wondered why you don't choose faith instead of worry, love instead of manipulation, or kindness instead of selfishness? Why don't we have a stronger appetite for God?

In this chapter we will discover that . . .

1. Our greatest natural desire is to be happy.
2. The most dangerous counterfeits of happiness are money, beauty, and talent.
3. God alone is the source of true happiness.
4. In our pursuit of God, we must guard our spiritual disciplines, our environment, and our friends.

I think there are two reasons. First, our appetites are shaped by what we consume. Second, what we consume is determined by our value system. Let's look at each of these.

First, our appetites are shaped by what we consume. When I was growing up, I ate Sugar Frosted Flakes for breakfast for many years. If it was morning, I ate Sugar Frosted Flakes. In college, I got hooked on Apple Jacks. After devouring bacon, eggs, toast, hash-browns and orange juice, I would eat three to six bowls of Apple Jacks each morning, depending on how hungry I was. I loved them.

A few years after my wife and I got married, we read of the negative effects of too much sugar in the diet, and so we weaned ourselves from so much sugar. Now, we have eliminated most of the obvious sugar in our diets. We don't normally eat desserts, we don't have a full sugar bowl in our house, and I don't eat sugar on my cereal. Instead of Sugar Frosted Flakes or Apple Jacks or Sugar Crisp, I now eat low-fat, organic granola which we make ourselves. I love it. I eat it for breakfast, for a snack each afternoon, and before going to bed at night.

Recently, a friend decided to cut out sugar on cereal, so we suggested Nutri-Grain Almond Raisin cereal. It can be bought in any grocery store, and from my experience, one of the tastiest and healthier commercially-produced cereals. Our friend tried it, and the next Sunday at church said, "That stuff tasted like *dawg* food." Now, if I had gone directly from my Sugar Frosted Flakes to Nutri-Grain, I might have thought the same. But I weaned myself off sugar gradually, and now the thought of sugar on cereal is repugnant. My point: our appetites are shaped by what we consume. Therefore, by changing what we consume, we can change our tastes, though it may seem flavorless at first.

To draw the spiritual analogy, few of us were raised on a meaningful relationship with God. Our tastes have been shaped by consuming all the things in life that substitute for fellowshipping with God. Fellowshipping with God is an acquired taste.

Now, to my second point: What we consume is determined by what we value. We have a natural desire for sugar. Babies like ice cream the very first time they try it. They don't have to learn to like it the way they do other foods. But many of the things we naturally like are not good for us—at least if used to excess. (Someone once said that the fact that broccoli is good for you and a hot fudge sundae is bad for you is proof that we live in a fallen world!) So we must force ourselves to do things that are not as pleasurable as those things we might more naturally do.

Margie and I cut back on sugar, not because we didn't like it, but because our value system changed. We decided we would rather pay the price of eating less sugar than pay the price of poorer health. Our value system determines what we consume and causes us to forgo the natural, immediate pleasure of sugar in order to gain the advantages of other, more healthful foods.

The spiritual analogy is that we must value the things God values. If we value them, we can choose to pursue them until our tastes change and we actually begin enjoying them. We *can* enjoy the things that are spiritually good for us.

What Is Our Greatest Natural Desire?

Our greatest natural desire is to be happy.

God created us with deep longings that drive our thoughts and actions. Different people express it in various ways, but our ultimate search is for happiness. We do the things we believe will make us happy.

People to Know

Blaise Pascal: (1623–1662) French mathematician, scientist and religious thinker; one of the greatest minds in Western intellectual history. His writings on religious subjects contain some of the most profound thinking in modern history.

C. S. Lewis: (1898–1962) British scholar and brilliant Christian thinker, writer, novelist, teacher at Oxford and Cambridge. His Christian books have sold more copies than any other author in history.

Blaise Pascal saw that

All men seek happiness. This is without exception. Whatever different means they employ, they all tend to this end. The cause of some going to war, and of others avoiding it, is the same desire in both, attended with different views. The will never takes the least step but to this object. This is the motive of every action of every man, even of those who hang themselves (*Pascal's Pensées* 113).

Some Christians have trouble accepting that, because we have this vague notion that it is not proper to want happiness. It sounds selfish. However, it may very well be that God created us for happiness. If so, it would not be wrong for us to want it. All that would remain would be for us to determine how we pursue happiness. If we pursue God and His purposes for creation, our longings will never be too great.

God created us with a deep desire for true happiness.

C.S. Lewis once wrote

that if there lurks in most modern minds the notion that to desire our own good and earnestly to hope for the enjoyment of it is a bad thing, I submit that this notion has crept in from Kant [a major German philosopher] and the Stoics [ancient Greek philosophers] and is no part of the Christian faith. Indeed, if we consider the unblushing promises of reward and the staggering nature of the rewards promised in the Gospels, it would seem that Our Lord finds our desires not too strong, but too weak. We are half-hearted creatures, fooling about with drink and sex and ambition when infinite joy is offered to us, like an ignorant child who wants to go on making mud pies in a slum because he cannot imagine what is meant by the offer of a holiday at the sea. We are far too easily pleased (*The Weight of Glory and Other Addresses*, 1–2).

Why Do I Need To Know This?

1. Unless you understand that only God can satisfy your fundamental drive to be happy, you could easily spend your entire life looking for happiness elsewhere.
2. You could not only out on happiness in this life, but on eternal life, also.
3. You must understand that desiring God is not enough. You must also stop doing the things that drive a wedge between you and God or else your relationship with Him will never flourish. It like physical fitness: Not only must you eat a good diet, but you must also stop harmful habits—smoking, drinking, worrying, stressing your body, and getting no exercise and too little sleep.
4. Unless you follow these principles, you will be of little help to others who are struggling. The ministry you long to have to others will not exist because you will not have any answers.

There is no vice in admitting our longings. We want to be happy. Now. How does that desire stack up with Scripture?

Happiness, or some other synonym that we might choose, such as joy, or meaning or satisfaction, is the sole intent of Christendom. Listen as the Scriptures speak.

> John 10:10 (Jesus is speaking of those who believe in Him): "I have come that they may have life, and that they may have it more abundantly."
> Matthew 5:8: "Happy are the pure in heart, for they shall see God" (NASB).
> Galatians 5:22: "The fruit of the Spirit is love, joy, peace. . . ."
> Psalm 37:4: "Delight yourself also in the Lord/And He shall give you the desires of your heart."
> Psalm 36:8: "[Men] drink their fill of the abundance of thy

house; and thou dost give them to drink of the river of thy delights" (NASB).

Psalm 34:8: "Oh, taste and see that the LORD is good."

Psalm 16:11: "In thy presence is fullness of joy; in thy right hand
there are pleasures forever" (NASB).

Happiness, joy and pleasure are not illegitimate experiences
in the Christian life; they are central to God's intentions. Most of
us have a right to be much happier than we are.

So step number one in the pursuit of God is to admit our
longings.

What Are the Most Dangerous Counterfeits?

The most dangerous counterfeits of happiness are money, beauty, and talent.

It is all right to desire happiness and joy. God created us with
those longings. But He also created us so that He is the only one
who can fulfill them. We err when we go outside of Him to try to
fulfill our yearnings.

Blaise Pascal went on to write:

> There once was in man a true happiness of which now remain
> to him only the dark and empty trace, which he in vain tries to fill
> from all his surroundings, seeking from things absent the help he
> does not find in things present. But these are all inadequate, be-
> cause the infinite abyss can only be filled by an infinite and im-
> mutable object, that is to say, only by God Himself (*Pascal's Pensées*
> 113).

We must deeply believe that God is the source of all true and
lasting happiness. We were created *by* God *for* God and we will
not find our happiness until we find it *in* God. Yet this takes us
180 degrees opposite our natural inclinations in our pursuit of
happiness.

What do we more naturally depend on to bring us happiness? Money is perhaps the number one thing. Beauty is another.
Talent is a third.

Money

Money gives status and brings power and freedom. Many of
you would say that you have difficulty thinking of anything you
need that money would not help. Perhaps you have been where I

have been before. I had my health. I had a wife who loved me. I had a job that I found meaning in. But if I just had more money! Everything would be perfect then.

Yet, money can be an opiate. It may be like cocaine. The more you have the more you may want, so that no matter how much you have, you still may not have enough. Therefore, money does not satisfy. Benjamin Franklin once said that:

> Money never made a man happy yet, nor will it. There is nothing in its nature to produce happiness. The more a man has, the more he wants. Instead of its filling a vacuum, it makes one. If it satisfies one want, it doubles and trebles that want another way. That was a true proverb of the wise man: rely upon it: "Better is little with the fear of the Lord, than great treasures, and trouble therewith."

In most cases, if you are not happy without money, you will not be happy with it. Money is often necessary for things we actually need, but if we look to it to make us happy, it fails us. As the source of happiness, even genuine money is a counterfeit—a mirage. Yet we all pursue and long for it perhaps more than anything else. But it is a starving substitute for God.

Money may help provide some basic needs, but it cannot make us happy.

Solomon said in the Proverbs: "Wealth is worthless in the day of wrath, but righteousness delivers from death" (11:4 NASB). "Do not wear yourself out to get rich; have the wisdom to show restraint. Cast but a glance at riches, and they are gone, for they will surely spout wings and fly off to the sky like an eagle" (23:4–5 NASB).

Beauty

We pursue beauty because we think that by looking nice, we can get people to like us. Now there is nothing wrong with looking nice. But if you are obsessed with it . . . if you are not content to look as nice as you do naturally . . . if you feel you must spend inordinate time and money to look nice, then you have a problem. And if you are so hungry for acceptance and love that you dress sensually, then you are setting yourself up for additional problems. Sensuality with our spouse is a delightful gift from God; but sensuality toward anyone else is always a trap—for all concerned. For everyone other than our spouse, then, we ought to dress in such a way as to draw attention to our face. It is the focus for all spiritual communication. So by dressing to emphasize our face (and to de-emphasize sexual sensuality), we are able to relate to people spiritually. We are able to concentrate on edifying speech, kind eyes, and gracious smiles, rather than tempting others physically with inappropriate dress.

If we are basing our happiness on people's acceptance of us because of how we look, we are setting ourselves up for disappointment. God has made us to look the way we look, and has done so for a reason. Therefore, He plans to give us a meaningful life no matter how we look. Our goal in life should not be to be so concerned with our appearance that we are willing to look or act unspiritually to gain others' attention. Our goal in life should be to ask God what it is that He wants to do in and through our lives, given the physical body He has given us.

Physical beauty always fades and cannot make us truly happy.

Beyond that, "looks" fade. Who among us over forty does not look back with some degree of wistfulness at the physical body he had ten and twenty years ago? This body is under the constant aging process and pull of gravity. It is deteriorating and is going to die. Building our life around how we look places us in bondage to a hopeless situation. It is like hugging a sinking ship. No matter what we do, eventually we all will be ugly if we live long enough.

Talent

Talent is similar to beauty. It is a wonderful servant or a terrible master. If we place our sense of worth on talents we possess, we become shallow and insecure, fearing the day our talent fails us. If we equate intelligence as a kind of talent, the same rule applies.

Only God can give us what we truly long for. In wanting money and beauty and talent, we are really longing for love and belonging, on one hand, and meaning and purpose, on the other. Only God can love us fully. Our spouse may fail us. Our family may misunderstand us. Friends may turn away. But God will never fail us. If we look to God to fund our emotional checking account, we can remain steady and strong when others fail us. If we are secure in God's love, our spouse can fail to love us, but we can keep on loving him or her. If we are secure in God's love, our family can misunderstand us, but we can keep on loving them. If we are secure in God's love, friends can turn away, but we can keep on loving them. Only God loves us fully, and He gives us the strength to love others in return.

And our spouse, family members, and our friends will die. But God will not die. If we are secure in God's love, we can remain unbroken when loved ones die, and while we may be terribly lonely, we can live in anticipation for the day we will be reunited with our loved ones, because God will bring it to pass.

Only God can love us perfectly and unendingly. Only God can meet our ultimate need for love and security and acceptance.

And as for meaning and purpose and satisfaction? Only God can give us that. What job gives us ultimate meaning and satisfaction? What accomplishment lasts? I remember when I learned that my first book would be published. I received the call from the publisher around noon. After I hung up, I jumped up and down in the middle of the room and shouted for probably two minutes. Then I did a jig and began skipping around the perimeter of the room. Finally, I danced into the middle again and repeated my original performance of jumping straight up and down, whooping and hollering.

> Talent, like money and even beauty, is a wonderful servant, but a terrible master.

That joy lasted for about a week. Then life resumed its usual course. Now that I have written a number of books, the thrill lasts for about ten minutes before the reality sets in.

What job will give you ultimate fulfillment? You work your head off and the people you work for don't appreciate it or reward you sufficiently. You give your money away to people, and they come to expect it. You pour your life into your children and they have no capacity to appreciate what you do for them. Don't get me wrong. It is right and good to take meaning in the things you do, but you cannot build your whole life on them. They will fail you.

But God—God doesn't fail you. The one thing that can give ultimate and permanent meaning in life is to know that when you go to bed at night, you lived that day, as best you knew how, for God. You served with your life the Creator of the universe, contributing to the great cause of the ages by living for God and living with God: "Today, I lived for God." If that anchors your life, the winds of adversity can blow and the vicissitudes of life can take their unexpected turns. It doesn't matter. You are anchored to a Rock that will not move. You are secure.

God may give us great meaning and satisfaction in people and in our jobs. He may have made us beautiful or handsome. We may get much fulfillment from life. But if we are not living for the Lord, we crash and burn when life fails us. If we are living for the Lord, we may crash, but we don't burn. We can rise again. We must recognize the counterfeits we live for; call them what they are, and live for the things which alone can give ultimate satisfaction.

What Is the Source of True Happiness?

God alone is the source of true happiness.

After we have admitted that we have a deep longing for happiness—a longing for love and acceptance and security on the one hand, and purpose and meaning and satisfaction on the other—we must choose things of true value, and reject things that are false.

When we feel lonely and rejected and yearn for someone to affirm us, it is heaven that we long for; it is God whom we seek. When we are tired and defeated and crave a taste of success, it is heaven that we long for; it is God whom we seek. When we seem hollow and empty inside, struggling for meaning and purpose in life, it is heaven that we long for; it is God whom we seek.

Surely, God will give us people and circumstances which help us from time to time to feel accepted and to have meaning in **Only God can** life. But what happens when all fails us? What **provide true** do we do when life collapses in on top of us? We **happiness.** have a protection. In the tempest we have safe harbor. In the darkest night, we have a compass. God will see us through if (and it is a big if) we have given ourselves to Him and have learned to take our love and purpose from Him. Life may hurt us, but with God in our hearts, it will not destroy us.

Listen to what Paul wrote in 2 Corinthians 4:8–10:

> We are afflicted in every way, but not crushed; perplexed but not despairing; persecuted, but not forsaken; struck down, but not destroyed; always carrying about in the body the dying of Jesus, that the life of Jesus also may be manifested in our body (NASB).

The price of choosing God, is, of course, total.
You may have heard the following story:

"I want this pearl. How much is it?"

"Well," the seller says, "it is expensive."

"But how much?" we ask.

"Well, a very large amount."

"Do you think I could buy it?"

"Oh, of course, everyone can buy it."

"But, didn't you say it was very expensive?"

"Yes."

"Well, how much is it?"

"Everything you have."

We make up our minds. "All right, I'll buy it," we say.

"Well, what do you have?" he wants to know. "Let's write it down."

"I have ten thousand dollars in the bank."

"Good. Ten thousand dollars. What else."

"That's all. That's all I have."

"Nothing more?"

"Well, I have a few dollars here in my pocket."

"How much?"

We start digging. "Well, let's see—thirty, forty, sixty, eighty, a hundred, a hundred twenty dollars."

"That's fine. What else do you have?"

"Well, nothing. That's all."

"Where do you live?" He's still probing.

"In my house. Yes, I have a house."

"The house, too, then." He writes that down.

"You mean I have to live in my camper?"

"You have a camper? That, too. What else?"

"I'll have to sleep in my car!"

"You have a car?"

"Two of them."

"Both of them become mine. Both cars. What else?"

"Well, you already have my money, my house, my camper, my cars. What more do you want?"

"Are you alone in this world?"

"No, I have a wife and two children . . ."

"Oh, yes, your wife and children, too. What else?"

"I have nothing left! I am left alone now."

Suddenly the seller exclaims, "Oh, I almost forgot! You yourself, too! Everything becomes mine—wife, children, house, money, cars—and you too."

Then he goes on. "Now listen—I will allow you to use all these things for the time being. But don't forget that they are mine, just as you are. And whenever I need any of them, you must give them up, because now I am the owner."

Choosing God not only costs all that we have. The price is all that we are. In return, God promises to fulfill the deepest longings of our soul. He promises to satisfy us with Himself.

We admit our deep longings, we recognize the inadequacy of counterfeits, and we choose God. That is the basis upon which we pursue God. In our great longings in life, ultimately, it is heaven that we long for. It is God whom we seek.

What Must We Guard in Our Pursuit of God?

In our pursuit of God, we must guard our spiritual disciplines, our environment, and our friends.

Engaging in "religious activities" is not the same as pursuing God. You can engage in religious activities with a heart of stone. Many people do. You can engage in religious activities with a heart inflamed with lust. Many people do. Participating in religious activities guarantees nothing. On the other hand, if you have a heart sensitive toward God or want to develop one, there are certain "religious-looking" activities you must engage in. Just because you do them doesn't mean you are pursuing God, but if you are pursuing God, you must do them.

We Must Guard Our Spiritual Disciplines

First, you must pray. The very heart of pursuing God is talking to Him. You should not only have regular times for prayer, you should cultivate a habit of going to God throughout the day in prayer as though you were conversing with someone at your side. Actually He is closer than that. He is within you.

Another thing you must do is learn your Bible. Notice I did not say read or study, because they are often too simplistic. You must read and study, but you must also hear good preaching and be involved in a Bible study with a good teacher. All four things, at least. Reading good Christian books, taking Christian study courses by tape or correspondence, and other similar activities help you learn your Bible. Jesus said, "You shall know the truth, and the truth will set you free." That means that if you remain ignorant of the Bible, you will be in bondage; bondage to bad decisions, foolish desires, to unhelpful attitudes, and so on. You must learn the Bible.

You must also worship with other believers. In most cases, this means going to church, though there are rare exceptions where that is not always possible. You may be a missionary in a Muslim country where there is no church to go to. But you can worship God nevertheless. The typical person in the United States, however, is **Spiritual disciplines help us pursue God.** spiritually obligated to find the best church he can find, connect with the most spiritual people in it, and try to make it an even better church.

Pursuing God means that you will attempt to live a life of service to others. There are those who are not Christians, and you can share the gospel message with them. There are those in need and you may be able to help in Jesus' name. Other Christians may need the benefit of your God-given gifts. Jesus said that if you would keep your life, you must lose it. He meant, primarily, that one must relinquish his life to the authority of Jesus, and implied that we must live for others, not merely for ourselves.

The Lord will give you many opportunities to pursue Him. If your heart is in pursuit, you will find a hundred disciplines to help.

We Must Control Our Living Environment

What does this mean in practical terms? For most Christians, it means turning off the television. Television militates against Christian standards, and especially affects children negatively. Over the last ten years of pastoring, I can often tell at a glance which children are raised on television and computer games, and which are not, and which have them carefully limited and supervised. Not only do television and computer **Our living environment may help or hinder our pursuit of God.** games damage directly, but they also keep children from and blunt their interest in more wholesome pursuits centered on relationships with people, reading, and nature.

Furthermore, just by occupying our minds so that we cannot think about God, television does enough damage. We don't have enough wholesome solitude (not to be confused with the seclusion encouraged by all manner of personal electronic entertainment products). We must turn off the radio and CD player for the same reasons. Those are the "sugars" that we must stop eating. We must begin eating the vegetables and low-fat granola of Scripture reading, prayer, meditation, Scripture memory, Bible studies and service with other Christians, church attendance, reading good books, developing relationships with people, and engaging in outdoor activities or those that use a particular talent or interest. Activities that develop the person and the gifts God has given him satisfy and give joy to life. Media entertainment, while not all bad, tends to develop nothing within. It merely occupies the mind while time passes, and often does so in a way that militates against Christian values. Turning off the television set may seem impossible or undesirable, but remember, our tastes can change so that we prefer the good to the bad.

We Must Control Our Relationships

The apostle Paul wrote in 1 Corinthians 15:33, "Do not be deceived: 'Bad company corrupts good morals.' " That is, the people we befriend influence us for good or ill. So we must choose our friends wisely. They can make us or break us.

The argument is often made that Jesus spent time with sinners, so why, then, can't we? We can, if we are spending that time for the right reason. While Jesus was surely great company, He never sacrificed God's standards for His relationship with sinners. Today, Jesus would not go with someone to an X-rated movie to gain an opportunity to witness to him. In doing so, Jesus would be violating His own moral standards, losing all credibility to anyone with spiritual sensitivity. However, He would go to that same person's home to talk with him about God, salvation, heaven, hell, and so forth, as well as enjoy wholesome "non-religious" conversation and leisure. Jesus interacted with sinners in a perfect blend of righteousness and warmth. Following this, our contact with sinners must be on the same gospel terms.

In our choice of friends, we choose who influences us in our pursuit of God.

If we sink to the level of those who are "bad company," it will corrupt our good morals. Therefore, we must be just as careful about our friends as we are the movies we watch, the music we listen to and the material we read. Anything that brings us closer to Christ is okay. Anything that takes us farther away from Christ must be jettisoned.

Conclusion

As I mentioned earlier, Margie and I have gone off desserts except for certain holidays and days that are special to us. One of those days is the Fourth of July. We wanted the freedom to have apple pie and ice cream with the rest of America on the Fourth of July. One Fourth of July we decided to celebrate by going down to a special restaurant for their five-nut brownie with vanilla ice cream on top. We dreamed of that dessert. We decided weeks ahead of time that we would get a bowl of baked potato soup and split it. Then we would get one of their special salads and split it. Then we would each get a five-nut brownie. We didn't want to be so full that dinner spoiled our dessert.

We ate the baked potato soup. It was all that we hoped for. We ate the special chicken salad. It was everything we remembered. Then came the five-nut brownie we had anticipated so long. We each got one. We looked at them for a second. We lifted them up and smelled them. We touched our tongues on the spoons and rolled them around in our mouths. Then, we dug in. Each of us took a big bite of brownie and ice cream, and, as we

As we pursue God, He will change our tastes.

swallowed, we almost choked. I gaped at Margie. Margie gaped at me. It was so sweet and so rich, it overwhelmed us. Not easily dissuaded, we pretended it wasn't really so bad, and we plowed into another bite. Our breath hitched. We almost gagged. Awash in denial and desperately wanting to enjoy it, we took one final bite. It was all over. We were defeated. We threw down our spoons. The five-nut brownies remained on our plate as we paid our bill and walked out the door. We went home and I had a bowl of granola.

As we pursue God, He will change our tastes. He will lessen our taste for the things the world finds enjoyable but not fulfilling. And He will satisfy us with Himself. Imagine that you are adrift in the ocean without any water. Drinking saltwater will dehydrate and eventually kill you. If you were adrift at sea without water, you would long to drink the water that formed the platform beneath you. But if you drank it, your platform would become your grave. The saltwater would kill you.

In that situation, it is not wrong for you to be thirsty. You were created to need water. You were created to develop a deep, driving thirst if you go too long without water. But you must drink pure water. To drink salt water does not satisfy the craving that drove you to drink it in the first place. Rather, it hastens your death.

And so it is with the emotional longings that drive so many of us. We long for love and acceptance, meaning and purpose. It is not wrong for us to long for them. We were created to long for them. God has created us to value these things. But He also created us so that He, and He alone, can satisfy these longings. Only in Christ can we have these longings gratified. We find ourselves adrift in life, floating on a sea of money, and sex, and ambition, and pleasure. We think that by drinking them, we will slake our thirst for love and acceptance and meaning and purpose. Not so. They are all saltwater.

Do you have unfulfilled longings in life? It is heaven that you long for. It is God whom you seek. Do not pursue these counterfeits that do not satisfy. Pursue God.

Speed Bump!

Slow down to be sure you've gotten the main points of this chapter.

Question
Answer

Q1. What is our greatest natural desire?

A1. Our greatest natural desire is to be *happy*.

Q2. What are the most dangerous counterfeits?

A2. The most dangerous counterfeits of happiness are *money, beauty*, and *talent*.

Q3. What is the source of true happiness?

A3. God alone is the *source* of true happiness.

Q4. What must we guard in our pursuit of God?

A4. In our pursuit of God, we must guard our spiritual *disciplines*, our *environment*, and our *friends*.

Fill In the Blank

Question
Answer

Q1. What is our greatest natural desire?

A1. Our greatest natural desire is to be _____.

Q2. What are the most dangerous counterfeits?

A2. The most dangerous counterfeits of happiness are _____, _____ and _____.

Q3. What is the source of true happiness?

A3. God alone is the _____ of true happiness.

Q4. What must we guard in our pursuit of God?

A4. In our pursuit of God, we must guard our spiritual _____, our _____, and our _____.

For Discussion and Thought

1. What is your area of greatest deception concerning happiness? That is, what is it that you are tempted to think will make you happy besides God?

2. Most Christians do not want an easy life instead of God. They want an easy life in addition to God. What is your greatest weakness when your life is not easy?

3. What is your greatest weakness to guard against, your spiritual disciplines, your environment, or your friends? What do you think you should do about it?

What If I Don't Believe?

1. I will be tempted to believe that happiness can be found outside of the pursuit of God.

2. I will be tempted to pursue what money, beauty or talent can bring me, rather than God.

3. I will grieve the Lord and impede my own spiritual relationship with Him because I do not consider Him and what He gives me at any given moment all that I need in life.

4. I will not be motivated to guard my spiritual disciplines, my environment, or my friends, to make sure they are not taking me farther away from God.

For Further Study

1. Scriptures.

Several passages will enhance the study of the pursuit of God and all that was discussed in this chapter. They include:

- Psalm 101:2–3

- Matthew 6:33

- John 10:10

- John 15:10–11

- Romans 12:1–2

- Galatians 5:22–23

- Ephesians 5:2–6

Read these passages and consider how they integrate with the material discussed in this chapter.

2. Books.

Several other books are very helpful in studying this subject. They are listed below in general order of difficulty. If I could only read one of these, I would read the first one:

Joy That Lasts, Gary Smalley
30 Days to Understanding How to Live as a Christian, Max Anders
Rediscovering Holiness, James I. Packer
Inside Out, Larry Crabb

When I have learnt to love God better than my earthly dearest, I shall love my earthly dearest better than I do now.
■ **C. S. Lewis**

9

What Does It Mean to Love God?

Hypocrisy is just about the worst sin an American can commit. Americans will tolerate immorality, dishonesty, and greed, but they hate hypocrisy. To be a "phony," or "hypocrite," is to sink to the bottom of the human ocean. And while there seems to be something a little hypocritical about tolerating immorality, dishonesty, and greed while being intolerant of hypocrisy, nevertheless, hypocrisy is a bad sin, even in the eyes of God. Jesus focused a verbal barrage at the religious leaders of his day concerning their hypocrisy. "Woe to you, teachers of the law and Pharisees, you hypocrites! You shut the kingdom of heaven in men's faces. You yourselves do not enter, nor will you let those enter who are trying to" (Matthew 23:13 NASB). This "woe" is followed by others that Jesus pronounces on the heads of the hypocritical religious. This is an official "Scathing Rebuke!" Hypocrisy is not something to indulge in.

On the other hand, we often appreciate the authentic, the real, as Pastor Bill Hybels explains.

American Novelist William Faulkner toiled for years as an unknown, unrespected writer in the rural Mississippi town of Oxford before he gained recognition. When he won the Nobel Prize for Literature in 1950, his acclaim grew. Approached later about the literary people and authors he associated with, Faulkner shrugged his shoulders and said he didn't know any literary people. "The people I know are other farmers and horse people and hunters, and we talk about horses and dogs and guns and what to do about this hay crop or this cotton crop, not about literature."

Faulkner was a "real person" who befriended real people. Unpretentious people. People honest about their life and living. He chose to surround himself with those who populated his stories and actually lived in his intensely human fiction, rather than those who simply talked about the South, or wrote about it.

I've often spent time with people who simply talked or wrote about Christianity. I'd much rather spend time with people who actually lived it. Too often, we Christians settle for unauthentic Christianity. (*Honest to God?*)

There is a compelling ring to those words, isn't there? There is an absence of hypocrisy in Faulkner's words. We all long to live authentic Christian lives and to hang around others who live authentic Christian lives. But we struggle with spiritual reality ourselves, and we have difficulty finding other Christians who live deep spiritual lives.

In this chapter we learn that . . .

1. We must obey God's commandments to demonstrate our love for Him.
2. God has given each of us the three basic resources of time, talent, and treasures, and we must commit those resources to Him.
3. How we love others is a test of how we love God.

As we review the quality of our Christian experience, we ought to ask ourselves from time to time, what does it mean to live an authentic Christian life? How can we keep from being hypocrites?

Chuck Colson, one of former president Richard Nixon's closest confidants but now head of Prison Fellowship, wondered the same thing after he became a Christian. He saw an American culture ravaged by a "me-first" mentality. The self-fulfillment fads of American culture had led to self-absorption and isolation, rather than to the fuller, liberated lives predicted. In *Loving God*, Colson wrote, "Three decades of seemingly limitless affluence have succeeded only in sucking our culture dry, leaving it spiritually empty and economically weakened. Our world is filled with self-absorbed, frightened, hollow people" (13). He then realized that the key to putting more into Christianity was in following the greatest commandment, which was to love the Lord your God with all your heart and all your soul and all your might (Matthew 33:37–40). But when he asked others what it meant to love God like that, he got different answers. In *Loving God* Colson champions a truly biblical understanding of what it means to love God. We want to do the same.

We need to de-mystify what it means to love God. We need to bring it down to an understandable level. We need to define it so that it is clear what we are to do, and so that we will know whether we are doing it.

I believe that every Christian would say that he wants to love God. But I also believe that we are not sure how to go about it consistently. I remember several years after I had become a Christian. I heard a fellow speak who was probably in his mid-fifties. He had a pleasant, perpetual smile. The joy of the Lord seemed to ooze out of him. As he was speaking, he used words like "precious," "sweet," and "glorious." "I came to know my precious Savior one glorious day twenty-three years ago," he said. "Every day that my lovely Lord and I have walked together has been dearer than the one before. I have not been out of fellowship one single day since that first glorious day."

I was dumbstruck! I thought that the guy was from Mars, or that he was superhuman—not like me at all! I had piled up an impressive number of days lived *out* of fellowship with God. Mind you, I didn't doubt his walk with the Lord. It was so far removed from my own experience that I wondered if we had anything in common.

As a result, I began to doubt the authenticity of my Christian walk. And this was compounded due to some songs I was learning. There was the song, "Sweeter as the Years Go By." The refrain went, "Sweeter as the years go by, sweeter as the years go by. Richer, fuller, deeper, Jesus' love is sweeter, sweeter as the years go by." That's a fine hymn, but the word "sweet" was not the word I would have used to describe my walk with the Lord. It wasn't a bad walk with the Lord. It was very meaningful, important, deeply significant. I just wouldn't have described it as sweet.

Another hymn, "Since Jesus Came Into My Heart," also troubled me. The refrain goes, "Since Jesus came into my heart, since Jesus came into my heart, floods of joy o'er my soul like the sea billows roll, since Jesus came into my heart." Now, I had had one or two sea billows in my short Christian experience, but I could not say that my life was a constant moving of the tide. Sea billows of joy *were not* perpetually washing over me. I began to doubt my walk with God because I feared that my Christian experience was inadequate. As much as I wanted and tried to love Him, I began to question whether I did love Him. So for me, as it may be for you, I had to find out what it meant to really love God.

Because of all this early influence and misunderstanding, it took me many years to get comfortable with what it means to love God in a biblical sense and to become convinced that I did love God. I want to share with you some of that journey through Scripture and through

---

Why Do I Need To Know This?

If I don't understand the role of obedience and emotions in loving God,

1. I am likely to misunderstand what it means to love God. The typical result is to focus on emotional experiences and pay less attention to the importance of obedience to His commands.
2. I may get frustrated and quit trying to love God because we cannot sustain sufficient ongoing emotional experiences.
3. I may never break my commitment to this world and as a result, never begin giving away money, time, and emotional energy to eternal causes.
4. I may never grow in my commitment to love other people.

---

life, in hopes that it may help you or someone you may be trying to help.

Let's begin describing what it means to love God with John 3:16, "For God so loved the world that He *gave* his only begotten Son." Also in Ephesians 5:25, we read, "Husbands, love your wives, just as Christ also loved the Church and *gave* Himself for her" (emphasis added). The fundamental characteristic of love is that it *gives*. Therefore, if we are to love God, we must *give* to Him.

But what does God need?

Nothing.

What does He want? Ah, there we strike pay dirt. In the Scripture we find three things clearly stated desires for God we may satisfy.

How Must We Treat His Commandments?

We must obey His commandments to demonstrate our love for God.

I heard a heartwarming story of obedience not long ago. An acquaintance told me that she and her husband were hoping to catch a few extra winks of sleep one Sunday morning, but they were having great difficulty because the kids were already up and in their parents' bedroom. The parents normally don't let their kids watch a lot of cartoons, but they thought it wouldn't hurt to relax the rule that Sunday morning, so they could get a little more sleep.

My friend and her husband eventually got up and went into the living room where the children were watching a television preacher. She was pleased at their choice, but curious, so she said, "Why aren't you kids watching cartoons?" One of her children said, "We were going to, but when we started to change channels, the preacher said, *'Don't touch that dial!'* So we're watching him."

Now that's obedience!

Obedience is a sign of loving God:

- John 14:15, "If you love Me, keep my commandments."
- John 14:21, "He who has my commandments and keeps them, it is he who loves Me."
- 1 John 5:3, "For this is the love of God, that we keep His commandments."

When I was coming out of the unhelpful early influences and misunderstandings described above, these verses became a big help to me. I had feared that only those who had a precious, sweet relationship with God were loving Him. Now I realized that I could love God even though I did not have a highly emotional relationship with Him. God does not want us to obey him on the level that we obey a drill sergeant. Rather than with gritted teeth and clenched fists, He wants us to obey him with an open heart and willing spirit, confident that that which He requires of us if for our good:

> **God wants our obedience to flow from trust in His goodness and love for Him.**

- 1 John 5:3, "For this is the love of God, that we keep His commandments. *And His commandments are not burdensome* (emphasis mine).
- John 15:10, "If you keep My commandments, you will abide in My love; just as I have kept My Father's commandments and abide in His love. *These things I have spoken to you, that My joy may remain in you, and that your joy may be made full* (emphasis mine).

So how do we obey God from the heart? It is when we come to deeply believe that everything God asks of us is something good for us, something to keep us from harm. Let's look, then, at three things which may keep us from believing that.

Barriers to Obedience: Ignorance

Sometimes we disobey God because we didn't know what is right to do. I got into some uncomfortable debts because I simply didn't understand biblical principles concerning finances. However, even though I was ignorant in that area, I paid a price anyway. Ignorance does not prevent consequences, though you might be tempted to say, "Well, that's not fair for you to pay that penalty if you didn't know what was right. And yet, if we were spared the consequences of sin simply because we were ignorant, I suspect it would make us want to increase our ignorance rather than our knowledge! The fact is, there are certain rules for temporal life, and if you break them you get burned. If you want to go to heaven, you must believe in and receive Jesus personally as your Lord.

Ignorance may prevent our heart-felt obedience.

If you want to live a rich, full life, you must adhere to the principles of living as found in the Scripture. Yet it is possible to obey one set of rules and not the other.

For example, there are church-going non-Christians, there are Mormons, there are New Agers, who follow the principles of living that we find in the Scriptures. As a result, many have fairly happy lives, even though they may not be Christians. On the other hand, there are Christians who are forgiven and redeemed, and headed for heaven, who, for one reason or another, do not follow closely the principles of Scripture, and who are miserable as a result.

Our great task, then, is to become a serious student of the Bible in order to believe with the heart that all of God's commands for us are for our good, to spare us unnecessary heartache.

Barriers to Obedience: Rebellion

Other times when we disobey, we know what is right and are capable of doing it, but we choose the wrong way. That is rebellion.

God deals patiently and compassionately with weaknesses like ignorance, but He deals strongly with rebellion. We see in 1 Corinthians 11 some people coming to the communion observances where they had a small, ceremonial meal, and eating all the food. They were gorging themselves with food that was supposed to be eaten in small measure, and they were not leaving any food for the others to take communion with. In addition, they were getting drunk on the communion wine, and in general, being dreadfully rebellious about an area of behavior which they could easily have controlled. As a result, some of the offenders were weak, and some were sick, and some of them even died. They were judged by God, and the judgment was significant.

Rebellion is a form of disobedience God judges firmly.

Parents know that their two-year-old is just that, and they are willing to deal patiently and compassionately with the child's weaknesses. They acknowledge that and accept it. But with outright rebellion, they have no choice but to discipline the child, as consistently as the rebellion warrants. The same is true with God and us.

Rebellion does not pay. If you are weary of feeling God's hand of discipline, you can repent and be restored to fellowship.

Barriers to Obedience: Lack of Trust

A third reason we don't obey God is that we may not really trust Him. Yet if He *is* good, loving, and just, then everything He asks us will be for our good. Since all His intentions for us are good, we would be foolish to disobey Him. It would be self-defeating, self-destructive, and counter-productive. When we disobey Him, chances are that we don't really trust His intentions.

When we think of obeying God, too often, we think of tight-lipped, grim-faced endurance of something that we ought to do, but don't want to do . . . something akin to taking bitter medicine. That is not the way it has to be. When we rest in His character, and power, and intentions, and take His word at face value, we can look forward to obedience. We can take refuge in obedience. We can obey, not with gritted teeth, but with relaxed heart. Whenever we find ourselves gritting our teeth in obedience to God, we are temporarily forgetting or overlooking, or failing to believe something good and true about Him.

> **Our failure to trust God's goodness toward us hampers our heartffelt obedience.**

Booster Toward Obedience: God's Truly Good Purposes

So, let's look at God's intentions for us, in order to confirm that everything He requires of us is for our good. In Deuteronomy 8:1–16, the Lord required the Israelites to obey Him in every situation because *He wanted to do good for them in the end*. Let us fix this truth in our minds. Even though it is not always easy to do things God's way, or painlessly, it is always right. Just as a surgeon has to "hurt" in order to heal, God must sometimes hurt, or allow hurt, for our own good. Is that a bad intention?

In Deuteronomy 6:24–25 and 10:12–13, we read that God gives us commands *for our good*. In Psalm 119:67, 71, 75, we see that it was *good* for David that God sent him trials. In Romans 8:28, we see that everything works together for *good* to those who love God and who are called according to His purpose. Goodness is God's intention for us. And the genius of God's system is that what He requires is what brings us to our highest good.

Does He ask you to be honest? It is for your good. It is harmful to you when you are not.

Does He ask you to be sexually pure? It is for your good. It is harmful to you when you are not.

Does He ask you to be ethical in your business dealings? It is for your good. It is harmful to you when you are not.

Does He ask you to be industrious? Does He ask you to be kind to others? Not to get angry? To be charitable in your finances? To forgive others? To be patient and loving and kind? It is for your good. It is harmful to you when you are not.

Surely, there are other reasons to obey God. Out of respect for Him. To be a good testimony to others. To contribute well to society. But in addition to all other reasons to obey God, it is best for you.

We only fool ourselves by thinking that we can take what we like of His commandments and ignore the others. Not all medicines meant to cure illnesses taste pleasant. We may refuse to take it, but what will the consequences be? That mindset leads to spiritual malnutrition. It keeps us from the full satisfaction we long for. It condemns us to a half-realized spiritual experience; we see what could be truer in our lives, but we don't experience it. We long for more, but we don't receive it. We are half-full glasses of water trying to overflow, and it doesn't work.

We don't have to be as miserable as some of us are. We don't have to live with as much pain as some of us do. But there is only one way out. His way. Not your way. Not half your way and half His way. But His way. Period.

God says "Be ethical in your business dealings." Are you cutting corners because you don't trust that God will take care of you?

You are dating a non-Christian, and people have warned you about it, but you are getting in deeper and deeper. Don't you trust God to take care of you in your loneliness and lack of purpose?

You are head over heels in debt. You are trapped into a lifestyle you can't afford. If one thing goes wrong, it will all come down around your head. But you won't get out. Don't you trust that God is sufficient to satisfy you? Don't you trust God to take care of you?

Don't do it—whatever it is that you are tempted to disobey God in. Stop. Remind yourself who He is. Remind yourself that He only loves you, and wants the best for you. Trust Him. Obey Him. You are the one who will suffer if you don't. And you will be the one to be blessed if you do.

Because it is impossible to keep all of God's commands in the forefront of our consciousness, let's reduce them to the five basic responses God asks of us. When you take all the commands and responsi- **God desires five responses from us.** bilities in the New Testament and put them into "like" categories, you will find five responses God wants from us:

1. To Love God

In return for loving Him, He wants to give us a satisfying relationship with Himself, the God of the universe. Everyone would long for spiritual intimacy with God if they knew who He was. He wants us to be deeply satisfied with Him (John 4:24).

2. To Love Others

In return for loving others, He gives us rewarding relationship with others. Our relationships with people help determine our quality of life. Everyone wants friends and a few very close friends. By loving others, we gain many friendships and a few close friends (Philippians 2:1–4).

3. To Esteem Ourselves

When we see ourselves as He sees us, we gain a satisfying relationship with ourselves. Most of us have a love/hate relationship with ourselves. We instinctively love ourselves but hate many things about who we are and what we have done. Yet God wants us to feel good about who we are in Christ, to experience the joy of seeing ourselves as He sees us. We are each priceless. If we believed that, it would free us of poor self-esteem. But no one person is of more value than another. If we believed that, it would free us of pride (Ephesians 1:3–4).

4. To Be a Steward

In return for being a steward, God frees us from the tyranny of pursuing "things" for their own sake. We hope that "things" will satisfy. "He who dies with the most toys wins," says the bumper sticker. But things don't satisfy, so God seeks to free us from the trap of living for them. He wants to free us from the bondage and futility and disappointment of living for this world (Ephesians 4:17–24).

5. To Be a Servant

In return for being a servant, God gives us a satisfying purpose in life. Man was not created to live selfishly, for himself only. He was created to live unselfishly, for others. Just as an eagle cannot be happy confined to a cage, so we cannot be happy confined to a life consumed with ourselves. As everyone lives for others, everyone's needs are met in a context of unity and harmony (Ephesians 4:11–16).

From these five examples we see that what He asks of us He intends for our good. When we believe that deeply, it gives us the capacity to obey God with a willing heart, even when the medicine tastes bad.

How Must We Treat Our Resources?

God has given each of us the three basic resources of time, talents, and treasures, and we must commit those resources to Him.

1. Time

You have just as much time as anyone else. And no matter how busy you are, there is always time to do the will of God.

God has given each of us three precious resources: time, talents, and treasures. Many of us neglect the will of God because we think we are too busy. We feel trapped by obligations, hemmed in by urgent requests, and overwhelmed by circumstances. Often, however, the way out is merely by rearranging our priorities. If something prevents us from doing God's will it is something that needs to be given up. We demonstrate our love for God by giving Him the time we should.

2. Talents

Each of us has been given spiritual gifts and personal abilities that God wants us to use for His glory as well as for our own pleasure. Yes, the things God has gifted us to do are things we enjoy doing. Many of us are not enjoying life as fully as we could be because we are not doing what God gifted us to do. It may be something for ministry, such as helping, or teaching, or counseling, or giving. It may be something like painting, or writing, poetry, or cooking, or something else. God has given each of us gifts and talents which He wants us to use to His glory, and when we use them to His glory we receive personal pleasure. So we can demonstrate our love to God by using our gifts and talents for Him.

3. Treasure

God has given each of us a personal treasure in our money. It is God who gives us the ability to make a living, and in some cases to prosper. Out of what He enables us to earn, He wants us to give some of it back to Him. Why? Because He needs the money? Not if He is the One who created silver and gold. Why, then? Because he uses it as a test to determine what we are living for. Are we living for self only, or are we living for God and the expansion of His kingdom? If the latter, we will manifest it by giving to that kingdom generously.

So, the one who loves God is the one who gives of His resources of time, talents, and treasures.

How Must We Treat Others?

How we love others is a test of how we love God.

In Matthew 22, someone in the crowd asked Jesus what the greatest commandment was. Jesus said it was to love the Lord your God with all your heart and with all your soul and with all your might. Then, he said that the second greatest commandment is like it. It is to love your neighbor as yourself.

Perhaps the best known principle in the Bible is the Golden Rule: "Do to others as you would have them do to you" (Luke 6:31 NIV). This is one of the most powerful sentences ever heard by man. It is the single-sentence answer to the majority of the suffering of mankind. First John 5:1–2 says, "Whoever believes that Jesus is the Christ is born of God, and everyone who loves Him who begot also loves him who is begotten of Him." First John 4:10–11 states, "In this is love, not that we loved God, but that He loved us and sent His Son to be the propitiation for our sins. Beloved, if God so loved us, we also ought to love one another." Finally, we read in 1 John 4:21, "And this commandment

Loving others is evidence that we love God.

we have from Him: that he who loves God must love his brother also." The final test of loving God is that we love others.

Conclusion

There it is. It is inescapable. Who loves God? The one who obeys His commandments. The one who gives out of his God-given resources. And the one who loves others. In isolating these three aspects, I hope we have de-mystified what loving God means. It is not being swept up regularly by emotion, feeling warm fuzzies toward God all the time. When feelings toward God come, that is certainly not to be despised. But sometimes you feel it, and sometimes you don't. Loving God, therefore, is about doing the right thing regardless of your emotional state.

In *Loving God*, Chuck Colson tells the penetrating story of a Russian doctor named Boris Kornfeld who was condemned to a concentration camp in Siberia because, as a Jew, he could not profess primary allegiance to the Soviet state, even though he was a confirmed socialist. The degrading and inhumane treatment at the prison camp stripped him of everything, including his idealism about socialism and his personal faith in God. Nevertheless, he met up with a Christian in the camp who shared Christ with him as the Jewish Messiah, and Kornfeld believed.

As a camp physician, Kornfeld had to sign death certificates for prisoners who were killed by the savage treatment they received. But on the certificate he was forced to say they had died of natural causes. Because of his faith in Christ, he finally refused to lie, and as a result the guards plotted his death. Kornfeld realized this, but having accepted the probability of death, he felt free to live. He signed no more papers or documents sending men to their deaths. He no longer participated in the evil system. And soon he realized that the anger and hatred and violence in his soul had vanished. He wondered whether there lived another man in Russia who knew such freedom!

Kornfeld longed to tell someone else about this new life of obedience and freedom. One gray day, Kornfeld began spilling his story to a cancer patient on whom he had operated. The patient missed the first part of the story because he was drifting in and out of the anesthetic. But Kornfeld's enthusiasm held the patient's attention, though he was shaking with fever. All through the afternoon and late into the night the doctor described his conversion to Christ and his newfound freedom. The patient knew he was listening to an amazing confession. Though the pain from his operation was severe, his stomach a heavy agony of molten lead, he hung on the doctor's words until he fell asleep.

The young patient awoke early the next morning, but the doctor did not come. During the night, while the doctor slept, someone had crept up beside him and dealt him eight blows on the head with a plasterer's mallet. The doctor was dead. But his testimony did not die. The patient pondered the doctor's last, impassioned words. As a result, he too became a Christian. He survived that prison camp and went on to tell the world what he had learned there. The patient's name was Alexander Solzhenitsyn (27–34).

Kornfeld was not going to lie, and he was going to testify for Jesus. Here was a Christian who, in the face of terrible odds, loved God from the heart. Ready to die for love of God, he shows us how to live out of that same love.

Speed Bump!

Slow down to be sure you've gotten the main points of this chapter.

Question **A**nswer

Q1. How must we treat His commandments?

A1. We must *obey* His commandments to demonstrate our love for God.

Q2. How must we treat our resources?

A2. God has given each of us the three basic resources of time, talent, and treasures, and we must *commit* those resources to Him.

Q3. How must we treat others?

A3. How we love others is a *test* of how we love God.

Fill In the Blank

Question **A**nswer

Q1. How must we treat his commandments?

A1. We must _____ His commandments to demonstrate our love for God.

Q2. How must we treat our resources?

A2. God has given each of us the three basic resources of time, talent and treasures, and we must _____ those resources to Him.

Q3. How must we treat others?

A3. How we love others is a _____ of how we love God.

For Discussion and Thought

1. Have you thought that in order to love God you had to have warm, emotional feelings about Him all the time? How has this affected your relationship with Him? How have you escaped that thinking?

2. If someone were to analyze your checkbook register and your credit card statements, what would they conclude about your relationship with God?

3. If someone were to analyze your weekly and daily schedules, what would they conclude about your relationship with God?

4. If someone were to analyze how you use your gifts and abilities, what would they conclude about your relationship with God?

5. If someone knew how you treated others, what would they conclude about your relationship with God?

What If I Don't Believe?

1. If you don't believe what it means to love God, you will be unlikely to take seriously the keeping of His commandments.

2. You will also be unlikely to commit your resources to the furtherance of His priorities.

3. There are many people who treat others well who do not love God. And there are those who say they love God who do not treat others well. Perhaps not all that much can be concluded by this criterion alone.

For Further Study

1. Scripture.

Several passages will enhance the study of the subjects of this chapter. They include:

- Psalm 90:12

- Matthew 25:15–28

- 2 Corinthians 9:6–7

- 1 Timothy 3:3

- 1 Timothy 6:10

- Hebrews 13:5

- 1 Peter 4:10

Read these passages and consider how they integrate with the material discussed in this chapter.

2. Books.

Several books are helpful in studying this subject further. They are listed below in general order of difficulty. If I could read only one of these, I would read the first one:

Loving God, Charles Colson
Knowing God, James I. Packer
Disappointment With God, Philip Yancey

*"Madame," I said, "if our God were a pagan
god or the god of intellectuals—and for me it
comes to much the same—He might fly to
His remotest heaven and our grief would
force Him down to earth again. But you know
that our God came to be among us. Shake
your fist at Him, spit in His face, scourge
Him, and finally crucify Him: what does it
matter? My daughter, it's already been done
to Him."*
■ George Bernanos, *Diary of a Country Priest*

Where Is God When It Hurts?

*T*he most difficult question people ask is, "Why does God not relieve
human suffering?"

The problem of human suffering and the apparent senselessness
of it is, perhaps, the single greatest dilemma people face with God. It
seems that either God is a bad trick played on man, or man is a bad
trick played on God. A perfect God and a suffering man don't seem to
go together. Rabbi Harold Kushner, who wrote *Why Bad Things Happen
to Good People*, said that anytime he gets into a discussion about religion, the conversation eventually turns to: "Why do the righteous suffer?" Dorothy Sayers once wrote: "The only question worth discussing
is 'Why do the righteous suffer?' "

How can God be good and still allow His children to suffer? "God,
how could You have let my baby die?" "How could You have let my
husband lose his job and our life savings, and his self-esteem?" "How
could You let me get into a terrible divorce when I tried so hard to save
the marriage?" "How could you let me languish in this physical pain?
Why don't you fix it?" "How could you let my wife die this slow, ex-
cruciating death from Alzheimer's disease?" "How *could* You?"

C.S. Lewis wrote these words in the midst of deep grief after his
wife's death from cancer:

> Meanwhile, where is God? This is one of the most disquieting
> symptoms. When you are happy, so happy that you have no sense of
> needing Him . . . you will be—or so it feels—welcomed with open

arms. But go to Him when your need is desperate, when all other help is vain, and what do you find? A door slammed in your face, and the sound of bolting and double bolting on the inside. After that, silence. You may as well turn away. The longer you wait, the more emphatic the silence will become (*A Grief Observed*).

Does God go away when we hurt? Does He bolt and double bolt the door of heaven when we are suffering? It is, as Lewis said, "the problem of pain." If God is all good and all powerful, why pain? Some people think that God must not be all good, which means that He

---

In this chapter, we learn that . . .

1. The most difficult question people ask is, "Why does God not relieve human suffering?"
2. Many realities in the spiritual world transcend human comprehension.
3. Jesus set the example of total trust and obedience to God, even in suffering.

---

doesn't really care about evil. Others believe that God must not be all powerful, so He can't do much of anything about it. When all is said and done, we may not understand God. Or we may not be able to reconcile evil with how God can be all good and all powerful. This means that we don't understand what His purposes are and how our ideals don't coincide with them.

Perhaps there are ways, however, to reconcile pain and God's character. As we've mentioned in a previous chapter, the Christian life is one of hope. Maybe the Bible will help us approach some answer for this universal human dilemma.

How Do We Reconcile Our Pain with God's Character?

We recognize that there are spiritual realities that transcend our comprehension.

Pain Is Universal

All people in all times everywhere have suffered. Certainly, some people have easier or harder lives than others, but suffering has always been a part of the human experience. This is true from the most primitive and godless cultures to the great people of the Bible. Joseph suffered terribly. So did Moses, David, and Daniel. So did Paul and James. What about Jesus? It should come as no surprise to us when we suffer. "Affliction does not come from the dust, nor does trouble spring from the ground; yet man is born to trouble, as the sparks fly upward" (Job 5:6–7).

We Lack Information

We can also assume there are reasons for our sufferings that we are unaware of. We may have to admit that we simply don't know. This goes back to the question of why God allowed sin to enter the world in the first place. That question has never been answered adequately. But since God is all good, there must be an explanation, which we cannot fathom.

There are many things about God that we are too little to carry. We just don't have all the information, or we don't have the ability to understand. There are millions of things I don't understand. For example, I cannot read a computer manual. I work on a computer all the time, but the only thing I can do is word processing, which is virtually "nothing" compared to what computers will do. People who fully know computers live in an entirely different world than I do. I will never forget the time I crashed my hard drive. This was the rough equivalent of hitting my computer on the head very hard, so that it forgot everything it ever knew. I had given it the wrong command, and it erased its memory. It first even asked me if I was sure I wanted to do that. But I was out in the ozone somewhere and said, "Yes." Obedient monster that it is, it immediately obliged and erased everything it knew. It forgot that I had ever entered and stored anything in its memory. I had two entire books I had written in the memory, as well as a lot of important information concerning the church I was pastoring. The screen went blank. I typed some stuff, and the screen remained blank. My computer was in a coma.

The effect on me was dramatic. I sat there in stunned silence trying to comprehend the significance of what had happened. For some time I was unable to admit that it had happened. Surely there was some way out of this. But, no. I had crashed my hard drive.

I left my office for a meeting where others were waiting for me. I lumbered into the room, slumped into my chair, and groaned the unthinkable, "Men, I've crashed my hard drive." A tense silence filled the air. Then someone ventured to speak. "Maybe you haven't lost everything. Maybe you have just lost the ability to get to everything." That is like saying, "Maybe your computer is not in a coma. Maybe it just has amnesia which a good doctor can correct." So I phoned the good doctor, "Magic Phil," who restored my hard drive. In several hours and for $250, the memory was back.

I wish I could explain to you how this man restored my computer, but I can't. I sat and watched him a while. Without a computer manual, he typed stuff that looked like "swearing" in the Sunday cartoons. No words. Just hieroglyphics. I say "without a computer manual" because to me it is like saying that he typed from memory the first twenty pages of the phone book.

I go to the lengths of telling this story, because it illustrates the fact that there are people who are far above us in intellectual power, and yet they are still human. There are people who know things that we will never understand. Maybe your weakness is literature, or plane geometry, or physics. The people who send rocket ships to the moon or who operate on the human brain are intellectually above the rest of us. Yet they are still only human. If there are humans who dwarf us intellectually, why should we be surprised if God dwarfs us intellectually? There are things which God knows, which make sense to Him, which we don't know or can't under-

We often lack satisfying information about our suffering.

stand. Accepting the finite limitations about our suffering is a second step in coping emotionally with the fact that pain exists, yet the Bible says that God is good and all-powerful.

How many times have you been puzzled by something, only to have it resolved later? You smack your forehead with the palm of your hand and say, "Ooohhhh. Of course." I am convinced that, when it comes to unexplainable suffering, the first sound most of us will hear in heaven is our hand smacking our forehead followed immediately by the surprised cry, "Ooohhh! Now I see!"

When on earth we cried, "Oh, God, when I was hurting, why didn't You heal me? When I was suffering, why didn't You come to my aid? When calamity was coming my way, why didn't You hear me? When I was alone, why didn't You visit me?" When we get to heaven, we will pause momentarily, and say, "Oh. Now I see."

Our second step is to assume that there is yet some information, some understanding, which we don't have.

We Lack Intellectual or Spiritual Ability

Next, we must accept that our ability to comprehend is limited. Let me tell you another story about Sugar Bear (please forgive me. She was just such a good source of illustrations). When she was about six months old, we began to try to train her. The first command was "Come." The book said that you were to say, "Come," and if she didn't come, you were to go get her and bring her to where you were when you said "Come" and that you were to do that in an enclosed space until she learned to come to you every time. Then you were to graduate to an open space. I don't know if that was the best way, but it did work.

We cannot fully understand what God is doing with us.

However, at first, Sugar Bear didn't understand what it was all about. She was intimidated by this change in her routine and this limitation on her freedom. She got apprehensive and insecure, and thought that we were unhappy with her. Her eyes clouded over and she became immobile. She feared the whole world.

"Why are they doing this? What have I done? Why don't they like me anymore?" her eyes seemed to be saying. We continued to love her and work with her, and the day came when she learned not only that command, but every other command which we needed for peaceful co-existence.

After she learned what we wanted and was reassured that we still loved her, everything was OK. But until that time, she was very unhappy. We had tried to explain to her: "This is not going to hurt you. We aren't angry with you. This is for your own good. This will make your life safer and better, and improve our relationship." Nothing mattered. She wanted out. Given the option, Sugar Bear would have bailed out of the learning process without a second thought. But we cared for her too much to let her. So we worked with her, and pushed through the apprehension and insecurity, and the result was a dog that was safer, more pleasant to be around, and had a better relationship with us. She was raised to a higher level of canine existence because of us.

Of course, the point is obvious. God works with us. But we cannot understand what He wants, and what He is doing. We get apprehensive and insecure. We may even get a little rebellious, as Sugar Bear did from time to time. We just don't have the ability to understand all that God is doing with us. But if we let Him, God will keep working with us, to push through the barrier, and raise us to a higher level of human existence.

We Must See Things From God's Point of View

While we cannot know all that God knows regarding our suffering, we can, however, learn to see things from God's point of view. God does not want to be your genie in a bottle. He does not want to be your cosmic vending machine. He does not want to be the solution to your equation. He wants a relationship with you. He wants you to know Him and to love Him. He has created the world so that nothing in our Christian life will work very well unless it forces us to deepen our relationship with Him.

Prayer won't reduce to an equation. Understanding how to live the Christian life won't reduce to an equation. Finding God's will won't reduce to an equation. If you are not doing what you can to get to know Him, paying attention to your successes and failures, learning how He works, and getting to appreciate Him, it won't work.

To understand what God is up to, we must go back to original creation. God describes in profound understatement what He did, in stages, and, after each stage, said, "It is good." When He finished with all the stages, He said, "It is *very* good." In Job we read, "The morning stars sang together and all the angels shouted for joy." Proverbs continues the buoyant mood: "I was the craftsman at his side. I was filled with delight day after day, rejoicing always in his presence, rejoicing in his whole world and delighting in mankind."

We can learn to see things from God's point of view.

"Oh, that their hearts would be inclined to fear me and keep all my commands always, so that it might go well with them and their children forever!" God cries. "Oh, Jerusalem, Jerusalem," Jesus lamented, "How I have longed to gather you to My self as a hen gathers her chicks under her wings, but you refused Me!"

God longs for an encounter with us. He longs for a relationship with us. He longs to know us and have us know Him. He longs to be intimately related to us. He longs for us to love Him, and to believe him, and believe *in* Him, and follow Him. In response, He promises untold blessings. Typically, like an undisciplined child or untrained dog, we won't follow Him completely enough, long enough to taste the blessings.

We get frustrated, or the pain gets too intense, and we begin to resent God. We clench our fists and grind our teeth and squint our eyes in rebellion. Why doesn't God fix our problems?

We have not yet begun to see things from God's point of view. From God's point of view, He is not out to get us, nor is He out to neglect us. He is out to make us like Him, and for reasons hidden deep in the mysteries of His will, He allows and uses pain.

However, God is not unaware or unaffected by our suffering. He does not leave us to suffer alone. He is not regaling the departed saints in a celestial party, oblivious to our plight, waiting for the day when we will finally join them. Rather, God is with us, always. When we hurt, God hurts. He feels our pain. He takes in all our pain. In some mysterious way, a God who is complete and lacks nothing links Himself with our suffering.

When it comes to God's identifying with our suffering, I have always felt that Jesus had credibility, because He came to earth and suffered for me far more than He asks us to suffer. So when He asks me to suffer, while I may not enjoy it, He has credibility with me. The Bible teaches that Jesus delighted to do the Father's will, but He did not delight to go to the cross. Scripture says that Jesus "endured the cross" (Hebrews 12:2). Luke 22:44 indicates that in the Garden of Gethsemane, Jesus was in emotional agony, and sweat profusely. Hebrews 5:7 says He cried. He asked for the

God our Savior fully experienced the pangs of human suffering.

help of friends who deserted him in Mark 14:32. He had to have angelic assistance to continue (Luke 22:43). Again in Mark 14, He said, "My soul is overwhelmed with sorrow to the point of death." So if Jesus asks anything of me, I feel a sense of fraternity with Him. Anything He asks me to suffer will be less than He suffered for me.

But I confess to struggling with God the Father. It always seemed unfair to me for God to be up in His celestial glory, untouched by the ravages of sin in the world, telling me to be patient, that it would all be over some day, and we'd get our reward.

However, as I searched the Scriptures, I discovered how wrong I was and how I missed the fact that anything Jesus the Son experiences is also experienced by the Father. God feels our pain. He takes it into His own heart. When we hurt, God hurts. Not only does he feel pain for us, but for all those on earth; and not only all those on earth, but all those who have ever been on earth, and all those who will be on earth. Those of you who are parents know how much pain you go through watching your children hurt. When they are in physical or emotional pain, your heart breaks with them. In the same way, God hurts when He sees us hurting.

Scripture says, "God was in Christ reconciling the world to Himself (2 Corinthians 5:19). Where is God when it hurts? He is on the cross, taking to Himself in Christ the pain, agony and terror of all the suffering of all the world for all time. As believers, we are united with Christ. When we suffer, God the Father suffers. When we are in pain, God feels and hears and cares.

No, God does not escape. He has chosen not to escape. Even from heaven, when I hurt, God hurts, and so I no longer cry out, "God, why don't you make it stop hurting?" He is hurting with me. In fact, we must not fail to marvel at how God's coming to us in Jesus the Son is the most potent way God could and did drink deeply from the bitter waters of human suffering. And so there must be a reason for suffering which lies beyond me.

> **God identifies with our suffering as the Creator who grieves over sin's carnage.**

I have been struck so many times when a parent takes a child to visit the doctor or dentist and the child either fears pain or feels pain. The child cries out from the bottom of his soul when the parent hands the child over to the doctor. Yet when it is all over and the doctor hands the child back to the parent, the child does not recoil from the parent for handing him over to such pain. Rather, sensing that there is some higher good, and sensing that the parent is hurting even as the child hurt, the child grabs the parent's neck, and buries his face into his shoulder, and at last is comforted.

We must try to see our suffering from God's point of view. He cares. He hurts with us. He obviously would prefer that we not suffer and promises that there will come a day when we will not suffer. But for reasons hidden in the mystery of His will, He has allowed suffering to come into creation . . . but with the suffering, He suffers, too.

We Must Believe that Our Suffering Matters

Obviously, then, our suffering matters to God. For instance, there is purpose behind it. In Hebrews 12:5–9, we read:

> My son, do not regard lightly the discipline of the Lord, Nor faint when you are reproved by Him; for those whom the Lord loves

He disciplines, and He scourges every son whom He receives. It is for discipline that you endure; God deals with you as with sons; for what son is there whom his father does not discipline? But if you are without discipline, of which all have become partakers, then you are illegitimate children and not sons. Furthermore, we had earthly fathers to discipline us, and we respected them; shall we not much rather be subject to the Father of spirits, and live? (NASB).

Yet there is a level on which we cannot see or know the reason. We cannot understand. When suffering comes on that level, we must trust, by faith, that it matters to God.

Why Do I Need To Know This?

1. If I don't know this, I may think that I am alone when I wrestle with why God doesn't relieve human suffering.
2. I may think there is something dreadfully unspiritual about myself if I'm angry with God about suffering.
3. I may feel alone and abandoned by God when I personally suffer.
4. I may not have a way of relieving the intellectual tension created by unexplainable suffering.
5. I may not realize that I need to study the life of Jesus to gain a better perspective on how to go through suffering.
6. I may not know how to appropriate the grace of God during times of trials.

In his book *Disappointment With God*, Philip Yancey writes about the "Great Wager." The Book of Job, Yancey wrote, is more than a book on suffering; it is a book about faith, the heart of which is the Great Wager in chapter 1. Satan wagers that if God takes away all blessing from Job, Job will curse God. God allows the wager. Yancey wrote:

When people experience pain, questions spill out . . . the very questions that tormented Job. "Why me? What's going on? Does God care? Is there a God?" This one time, in the raw recounting of Job's travail, we, the onlookers . . . not Job . . . are granted a view behind the curtain. What we long for, the prologue to Job provides: a glimpse into how the world is run. As nowhere else in the Bible, the book of Job shows us God's point of view, including the supernatural activity normally hidden from us.

Job has put God on trial, accusing him of unfair acts against an innocent party. Angry, satirical, betrayed, Job wanders as close to blasphemy as he can get . . . just to the edge. But Chapters 1 and 2 prove that, regardless of what Job thinks, God is not on trial in this book. Job is on trial. The point of the book is not suffering: Where is God when it hurts? The prologue dealt with that issue. The point is faith: Where is Job when it hurts? How is he responding? (165)

Yes, there was a wrestling match in Job, but it was not between God and Job, it was between God and Satan, although . . . most significantly . . . God had designated the man Job as His stand-in. The first and last chapters make clear that Job was unknowingly performing in a cosmic showdown before spectators in the unseen world (168).

Elihu, one of Job's accusers, said, in essence, "Job, you must have sinned terribly to have brought this suffering down on your head." Elihu was flat wrong, however. The opening and closing chapters of Job prove that God was greatly affected by the response of one man and that cosmic issues were at stake.

"The 'Wager' offers a message of great hope to us all," Yancey concludes. "Perhaps [it is] the most powerful and enduring lesson from Job. In the end, The Wager resolved decisively that the faith of a single human being counts for very much indeed. Job affirms that our response to testing *matters*. The history of mankind . . . and, in fact, my own individual history of faith . . . is enclosed within the great drama of the history of the universe" (170).

The Bible hints that something like that may be happening to us when we suffer. The suffering which we go through which makes no sense to us all is perhaps a cosmic drama in which we are not alone, though in our pain we feel very much alone. Perhaps at that moment when we feel most alone, most abandoned, perhaps at that very moment the eyes of heaven and hell are focused most **Our suffering matters.** sharply on us, to witness our faith and the triumph of God's grace. Thus, when we feel most removed from reality and purpose, we may be the most involved in them.

Sometimes God does give us a glimpse behind the veil. In my book *30 Days to Understanding How Christians Should Live*, I wrote about a lady in a church I pastored. Her husband, a school teacher, had applied for the unusual position of going into space aboard a NASA space shuttle. He had all the prerequisites. He was bright, well educated, an excellent communicator, a popular teacher, and so on. Their excitement grew as they envisioned that he might be the first non-astronaut in space. From the wife's point of view, it was not even really the possibility. It was the probability. There was no one more qualified than her husband.

While their hopes were at their highest, they were abruptly and cruelly shattered. A technicality beyond their control prevented getting the extensive application in on time. In the most favorable scenario, it would be one day late. No, there could be no extension; no late papers, as it were. No, they would not be granted an exception. No, he would not be the first non-astronaut into space, not because he was not qualified but because the application would be one day late.

The lady who told me this story was crushed, devastated, angry with God. It was a bone that stuck in her throat. She couldn't get over it until the day of the launch, that is. Watching the *Challenger* on television lift off and surge into that brilliant, cloudless blue sky, she said aloud, "That could have been my husband. God, how dare you!" The moment the words passed her lips, the *Challenger* exploded in a ball of flame, divided like a huge smoke wishbone, and dropped lifelessly to the ocean below. Everyone on board had died. She fell backwards onto her bed, shaken to the core.

We are not usually given glimpses behind the scenes like this. But it strikingly helps us see that there is more going on than meets our eye. What we see is not all there is. Our thoughts do not encompass all information. Therefore, we must always hope in God, and trust His actions, His timetable, His providence.

When you suffer, take strength. Take encouragement. Your life matters. It counts. God knows you. He loves you. He has not abandoned you. You are not alone. When you hurt, He cares. When you are lonely, He cares. When you are confused and fearful, He cares. He is not off in a corner of the universe paying attention to something that really matters. He is living within your heart, calling and hoping that your faith will remain strong in the struggle. And, He promises to set all things straight one day. What a celebration that will be!

How Is Jesus Our Example in Suffering?
Jesus set the example of total trust and obedience to God, even in suffering.

We can look to Jesus for an example of how we can endure suffering. When He was on the cross, he cried out, "My God, My God, Why hast Thou forsaken me?" This is a quote from Psalm 22:1–3:

My God, my God, why has Thou forsaken me?
Far from my deliverance are the words of my groaning.
O my God, I cry by day, but Thou dost not answer;
And by night, but I have no rest.
Yet Thou art holy,
O Thou who art enthroned upon the praises of Israel (NASB).

In this remarkable passage, we see the psalmist David, crying out prophetically, because he feels utterly forsaken. He says that both day and night he cries out, but God does not answer him. Yet without any explanation for God's silence, the psalmist affirms the holiness of God: "Yet, Thou art Holy. . . ."

Ultimately, our suffering may drive us to only this confession. We are free to cry to God. We may get no relief. We may get no answer. Yet God is still holy.

Again, Jesus provides an example for us as recorded in 1 Peter 2:20–24:

For this finds favor, if for the sake of conscience toward God a man bears up under sorrows when suffering unjustly. For what credit is there if, when you sin and are harshly treated, you endure it with patience? But if when you do what is right and suffer for it, you patiently endure it, this finds favor with God. For you have been called for this purpose, since Christ also suffered for you, leaving you an example for you to follow in His steps, who committed no sin, nor was any deceit found in His mouth; and while being reviled, He did not revile in return; while suffering, He uttered no threats, but kept entrusting Himself to Him who judges righteously; and He Himself bore our sins in His body on the cross, that we might die to sin and live to righteousness; for by His wounds you were healed (NASB).

Jesus simply took it, trusting in God to get Him through it, and trusting that in the end all would be well. No matter how hard, God will see you through it, and in the end all will be well. Trust also sustained the martyrs whose sufferings are described in the remarkable book, *Foxe's Book of Martyrs*. It tells story after story of early Christians who were martyred for their faith. Hebrews 11 says the world is not worthy of such people. In the providence of God, He calls some to higher degrees of suffering than others, and in the end, when all suffering for God's people will end, they will stand before the Lord and the hosts in heaven, and it will be declared to all the celestial hosts, "The world was not worthy of them!"

Speed Bump!

Slow down to be sure you've gotten the main points of this chapter.

Question **A**nswer

Q1. What is the most difficult question people ask?

A1. The most difficult question people ask is, "Why does God not *relieve* human suffering?"

Q2. How do we reconcile our pain with God's character?

A2. We recognize that there are spiritual realities that *transcend* our comprehension.

Q3. How is Jesus our example in suffering?

A3. Jesus set the example of *total* trust and obedience to God, even in suffering.

Fill In the Blank

Question **A**nswer

Q1. What is the most difficult question people ask?

A1. The most difficult question people ask is, "Why does God not _____ human suffering?"

Q2. How do we reconcile our pain with God's character?

A2. We recognize that there are spiritual realities that _____ our comprehension.

Q3. How is Jesus our example in suffering?

A3. Jesus set the example of _____ trust and obedience to God, even in suffering.

For Discussion and Thought

1. When you compare yourself with people who have suffered a great deal physically or emotionally, have you really suffered much? How would you assess the degree to which you have suffered in life compared to other Americans, or to Third World countries, or places where persecution occurs?

2. If you have not suffered a great deal, do you find yourself complaining about whatever is the most unpleasant thing in your life, even if it is trivial by comparison? How do you think you could change your attitude on this?

3. If you have suffered, have you found a measure of help in the things in this chapter or did you already know them? What has helped you the most?

4. What Scripture passages have been most helpful to you in coping with suffering?

5. How has the example of Christ helped you cope with suffering?

What If I Don't Believe?

1. If I don't believe this information about suffering, I may find myself suffering and not have any internal strength to deal with it.

2. I may get angry with God and be tempted to abandon Christianity.

3. I may find that I have no capacity to comfort others who are suffering.

For Further Study

1. Scriptures.
There are a number of passages on suffering which will give greater insight into the matter.

- Romans 8:18

- 1 Corinthians 12:26

- 2 Corinthians 4:16–18

- Galatians 3:4

- James 1:2–4

- 1 Peter 2:20–24

- 1 Peter 4:13

Read these passages and consider how they integrate with the material discussed in this chapter.

2. Books.
There are several helpful books for studying this subject further. They are listed below in general order of difficulty. If I could read only one of these, I would read the first one:

You Gotta Keep Dancing, Tim Hansel
Where Is God When It Hurts, Philip Yancey
Disappointment With God, Philip Yancey
A Grief Observed, C.S. Lewis
The Problem of Pain, C.S. Lewis

God weeps with us so that we may one day
laugh with Him.
■ Jürgen Moltmann

11

How Do We Cling to God?

There were times when things were going so badly for the prophets of the Old Testament that they could do nothing but cling to God. There were times when things were going so badly for the twelve disciples that they could do nothing but cling to God. There were times when things were going so badly for the apostle Paul that he could do nothing but cling to God. And there were times when things were going so badly for Jesus Himself that He could do nothing but cling to God.

We hear much about the peace, love, and the joy of the Christian life, and rightly so. These are promised to us as fruit of living under the guidance and blessing of the Holy Spirit. Also, most of us do not have as much peace, love, and joy as God intended us to have, so it seems appropriate that we should be taught how to experience these things more fully. On the other hand, if there were times when things were going so badly for the prophets of old, for the twelve disciples, for the apostle Paul, and for Jesus Himself, so badly that they could do nothing but cling to God, then it should not surprise us that we will have seasons like that.

When Jeremiah was called by God to be His prophet, God promised to take care of him. In Jeremiah 1:17, 18, we read, "I have made you this day a forti- **Biblical characters clung to God.** fied city and an iron pillar, and bronze walls against the whole land. . . . [The kings, princes, priests, and people] will fight against you, but they shall not prevail against you. For I am with you," says the Lord, "to deliver you."

But what happened? Was everything peaceful and cheery afterward? You probably know the story. The nation turned a deaf ear to his preaching, they plotted against his life, he was imprisoned, and in one incident, rebellious Israelites buried him neck deep in mud! What happened to the fortified city? What happened to the pillar of iron? Where were the walls of bronze? Where was God? Had God forsaken him? Had God's promises failed? No. The people did fight against Jeremiah, but they did not overcome him. God delivered him in the end. It is just that there were times when circumstances looked unpromising, and Jeremiah had nothing to do but cling to God.

This weighed heavy on Jeremiah. He doesn't deny the pain but clings to God. In Lamentations (written by Jeremiah) we read in 3:1–2, 7–9, 21–24:

> I am the man who has seen affliction because of the rod of His wrath. He has driven me and made me walk in darkness and not in light. He has walled me so that I cannot go out; He has made my chain heavy. Even when I cry out and call for help, He shuts out my prayer. He has blocked my ways with hewn stone; He has made my path crooked. This I recall to my mind, therefore, I have hope. The Lord's loving kindnesses indeed never cease, for His compassions never fail. They are new every morning; Great is Thy faithfulness. The Lord is my portion, says my soul, Therefore I have hope in Him. The Lord is good to those who wait for Him, to the person who seeks Him (NASB).

When God revealed Himself to Saul of Tarsus on the Damascus road, God promised him that he would become an apostle to the Gentiles. This must have been a time of great hope for Saul, but he was blinded by the terrifying encounter. Three days later, with no reason to think that he would regain his sight, a man sent by Jesus came to Saul and told him who Jesus was. Saul believed in Him, regained his sight, and went on to become the apostle Paul. But there were times during his ministry when things began going so bad for Paul that all he could do was cling to God. In Lystra the people rioted, hauled Paul to the edge of the city, stoned him, and left him for dead. Worshippers of Diana in Ephesus rioted because of Paul's preaching, and an ugly mob was rooting around the city looking to kill him. There were times when Paul was imprisoned, dealt with by a kangaroo courts, shipwrecked, almost drowned in a violent sea, and bitten by a poisonous snake.

Paul chronicled his misfortunes in 2 Corinthians 11:24–27:

> Five times I received from the Jews thirty-nine lashes. Three times I was beaten with rods, once I was stoned, three times I was shipwrecked, a night and a day I have spent in the deep. I have been on frequent journeys, in dangers from rivers, dangers from robbers, dangers from my countrymen, dangers from the Gentiles, dangers in the city, dangers in the wilderness, dangers on the sea, dangers among false brethren; I

have been in labor and hardship, through many sleepless nights, in hunger and thirst, often without food, in cold and exposure (NASB).

These were times when things were going so bad for Paul that all he could do was cling to God.

And Jesus, Himself, the evening before His crucifixion in the Garden of Gethsemane, was in severe distress. As the apostle Luke (22:43, 44) records it, Jesus knelt down and prayed, and "an angel appeared to Him from heaven, strengthening Him. And being in agony He prayed more earnestly. Then His sweat became like great drops of blood falling down upon the ground." The apostle Matthew (26:39) records that Jesus was so grieved and distressed about facing His death that he prayed, "O My Father, if it is possible, let this cup pass from Me; nevertheless, not as I will, but as You will." In that concluding phrase, we see that Jesus could do nothing but cling to God.

In this chapter, we learn . . .

1. How to cling to God in the midst of physical or emotional pain.
2. How to cling to God when we are spiritually dry.
3. How to cling to God when we don't know what God's will and we do not sense guidance that we feel we need.

As He hung naked on the cross hours later, in abject shame, but in even greater physical pain, His moment of ultimate trial came. The sin of the world was placed on Him, and He cried out, "My God, my God, why hast Thou forsaken me?" What a terrible time. No one could do anything for Him, and His circumstances could not be altered. There was nothing for Him to do but cling to God.

When you find yourself in distressing circumstances, you have two choices. You can chuck God, or you can cling to Him. If you chuck Him, you still have the distress, but you have no spiritual comfort from Him. If you cling to Him, you still have the distress, but you have the possibility of spiritual comfort from Him. Never give up. Never. Cling to God.

How Do We Cling to God When It Hurts?

When we are in pain, we must trust the Scriptures and use the pain to force us closer to God rather than drive us farther from Him.

Three common circumstances often force us to cling to God. The first is during terrible physical or emotional pain. It may be the physical pain of disease, or from an accident, or even deep nausea or just a hard to describe terrible feeling. It is a great cross to bear. Or it may be emotional pain, like the pain of fear, or anger, or bitterness, or loneliness, or rejection, or disappointment, or black unrelenting depression.

Sometimes, physical or emotional pain gets so intense that the only thing we can do is cling to God. As we saw above, in the Garden of Gethsemane Jesus was in horrible anguish about his death. What level of emotional pain would it take to cause the body to sweat great drops of blood? Apparently that happens when deep emotional stress causes the capillaries near the surface of the skin to rupture, and blood, perhaps mixing with perspiration, came sweating out.

The apostle Paul had some kind of problem which we don't fully understand. In 2 Corinthians 12:7–10, Paul described something which he calls a thorn in the flesh and a messenger from Satan to buffet him. Was it a physical malady, or was it spiritual suffering? My guess is both, perhaps a physical ailment caused by demonic attack. Whatever it was, Paul prayed three times for the Lord to remove it. The Lord didn't remove it. He simply said, "My grace is sufficient for you."

If God's grace is sufficient for Jesus and Paul, I would have to say that it is also sufficient for us as we tread life's troubled waters. Our measure of grace may not at times be enough for us to go water skiing but simply to keep our nostrils above the surface. Or, if we sink below the surface, it will be enough to bring us back up to keep from drowning. In fact, many people testify about times when His grace did not seem to be sufficient, but later they admitted that it was.

My wife and I have a friend who was in labor with her first child for nearly twenty-four hours. She was in the hospital most of that time in terrible physical anguish, which began to affect her emotions and mental stability. Suddenly she jumped out of bed and began throwing her clothes into her suitcase. Her husband yelled, "Susan! (Not her real name.) What are you doing?" She said, "I've had it. This is ridiculous. It is unreasonable to think a person should have to go through this, and I am not going to do it. I'm going home!"

Well, it took some persuading, but she got back in bed, had the baby, and eventually was able to laugh about it. But at the time, it was not funny. The pain and emotional distress became so

great she cracked. It did not seem like the grace of God was sufficient for her. Yet, here she is, alive and healthy,
and so is her child. The grace of God was sufficient for survival. But not for "Easy Street."

Pain forces us to cling to God

The Psalmist cried to God in the Psalm 22:

> My God, my God, why hast Thou forsaken me? Far from my
> deliverance are the words of my groaning. O my God, I cry by day,
> but Thou dost not answer; And by night, but I have no rest. . . . I
> am poured out like water, and all my bones are out of joint; My
> heart is like wax; it is melted within me. My strength is dried up
> like a potsherd, and my tongue cleaves to my jaws; and thou dost
> lay me in the dust of death (verses 1–2, 14–15, NASB).

In this intensely intimate cry of the soul, we see the Psalmist
simply clinging to God. There is no railing against God. There is
no questioning. It is simply the cry in the night of a hurting and
fearful child to his parent. Sooner or later, help will come. In the
meantime, there is nothing to do but cling to God.

To cling to God when it hurts, in spite of the pain, is to keep
on trusting. You cry for relief. You find means of grace for easing
the pain from any legitimate source, such as medication or mental exercises for physical or emotional pain, the help of friends,
good books to read, solitude or forms of diversion. Prayer, of
course, should be a constant. Through it all, you cling to God.

How Do We Cling to God When We Are Spiritually Dry?

*We must believe that the drought will eventually end and we must continue
to be faithful to the spiritual disciplines.*

A second time we must cling to God is when we go spiritually dry. Just as sun spots are said to cause a sixty-year cycle of
drought in the cornfields of Indiana, so there seem to be cycles of
spiritual drought in the lives of Christians.

These droughts may be minor periods of spiritual dustiness,
or they may be major league droughts, when the soil of the soul
dries and cracks like fissures on the desert floor. During periods
of dryness, we must do least three things. We must acknowledge
that the dryness is not permanent. Rain will come again. Life and
growth will return. God has not forgotten you. Remember what

Jeremiah said: "This I recall to my mind, therefore, I have hope. The Lord's lovingkindnesses indeed never cease, for His compassions never fail. They are new every morning; Great is Thy faithfulness. The Lord is my portion. Therefore, I have hope in Him." Keep on believing that the drought will end. It will.

Second, be on guard for things you may do to bring on the spiritual drought yourself. Insurance companies put out stress evaluation surveys to rate a person's chance of getting sick. If you have certain things happen to you, you rate them with a numerical value and then total them up to see what your overall stress impact is. For example, if you have moved recently, that equals so many points. If a loved one has died, that is so many points. If

Your spiritual drought will end. you have been physically ill for more than a week, so many points, and so on. A financial setback, a divorce, a change of jobs, all of these have stress values, and after going through the entire survey you add up your total to see the likelihood of getting sick from stress.

According to that chart, I should have died two Christmases ago. Circumstantial turmoil takes its toll and induces, in many instances, spiritual dryness.

Other factors which directly affect your spiritual vitality are: how many hours you work, how much sleep you get, how much television you watch, how much radio you listen to, and whether you smoke, drink alcohol, drink coffee or other caffeinated beverages, how much sugar you consume, how balanced your diet is, and how much exercise you do. Monitoring your lifestyle can give significant insight into things that might tend to induce spiritual dryness.

Third, pay attention to spiritual disciplines. When under prolonged intense suffering, we can sometimes lose our grip on spiritual disciplines like prayer, meeting with Christian friends, counseling, Scripture reading, even the laying on of hands by elders. I learned the hard way that when you slack off on these disciplines, you drop your guard against temptations.

I'm thinking about the summer after I graduated from college. It was a time of much stress. And besides that, the Holy Spirit was hounding me about some sins He wanted me to give up, and I wanted to give up, but wasn't having much luck. I was worried about all the money I owed in college loans, and about how I would ever go on to seminary. My father was dying from cancer, and I was selling books door-to-door in a faraway place.

Furthermore, I was not cut out for that job, and the hourly rejection was more than I could handle. In addition, the guys I lived with were some of the most negative, exasperating people I have ever spent time around. And because I was the one who had the car, I was playing nursemaid and taxi driver to them. Finally, though I was making a lot of money, I cracked. I scribbled a note telling the guys I was going home, and I left town. On the way home, near dark, I pulled into a drive-in theater and watched the dirtiest movie I could find.

Why did I do that? I had never seen a dirty movie before, and I was always careful to memorize Scripture and refrain from watching or listening or reading things that weren't edifying. It was not normal for me to do such a sinful thing. But I did it. I was so stressed out that the devil had his way.

You, too, might fall into temptation as a result of losing your grip on Christian disciplines. You might not be tempted to go to a dirty movie. You might be tempted to get drunk, or take drugs, or have an affair, or steal money, or run away. Whatever your weakness is, find someone who will help you through it, and cling to God.

You may not feel like praying, and when you pray, you may not "get anything out of it." However, you can say, "God, I don't feel like praying, and so I am praying out of obedience to You. Therefore, accept this emotionless time as an act of love to You." That is valid in times of spiritual drought.

Why I Need to Know This

1. If I don't know this, I may think that there is something wrong with me for not being able to escape my pain or deal more effectively with it.
2. I may feel that I would be better off if I just had more faith.
3. I might do exactly the wrong thing in trying to deal with my suffering.
4. I might be tempted to give up when there is still hope.

In his book *The Spirit of the Disciplines*, Dallas Willard writes:

We *can* become like Christ in character and in power and thus realize our highest ideals of well-being and well-doing. That is the heart of the New Testament message. We do it by following him in the overall style of life he chose for himself. If we have faith in Christ, we must believe that he knew how to live. We can, through faith and grace, become like Christ by practicing the types of activities he engaged in, by arranging our whole lives around the activities he himself practiced in order to remain constantly at home in the fellowship of his Father. What activities did Jesus practice? Such things as solitude and silence, prayer, simple and sacrificial living, intense study and meditation upon God's Word and God's ways, and service to others.

We must develop a counterculture mentality. I do not mean this in the sense that we wear plain clothes, drive horses and buggies, shun electricity, or get "back to nature." I find nothing wrong with those things, personally, if you choose them. I do not think they are necessary to develop a counterculture mentality, however, by which I mean that we embrace a lifestyle different than the world's. We choose to be Christian, and if that means we do not act like other Americans, then we do not act like other Americans. So, by counterculture, I do not have in mind physical but spiritual differences between Christians and the status quo.

For example, our culture does not put a premium on solitude, rest, prayer, or meditation. Thus in his book *Ordering Your Private World*, Gordon MacDonald has written:

> I get the feeling we are a tired generation. Evidence of that fatigue abounds in a multitude of articles about health problems related to overwork and exhaustion. Why is there so much exhaustion and fatigue today? One reason is that we are not following the biblical view of rest. Resting properly is a key to ordering our private worlds. Rest was not meant to be a luxury, but a necessity. By rest, I do not mean amusement. Although [amusements] may provide a sort of momentary rest for the body, they will not satisfy the deep need for rest within the private world.

Again, the psalmist wrote about his own time of spiritual dryness. In Psalm 63:1, we read, "O God, my God, I shall see Thee earnestly; my soul thirsts for Thee, my flesh yearns for Thee in a dry and weary land where there is no water."

When David was spiritually dry he simply told God that he was spiritually dry. But we see from his worship, even then, that he clings to God. Notice Psalm 63:2–3 and 6–8:

> Thus I have beheld Thee in the sanctuary, to see Thy power and Thy glory. Because Thy lovingkindness is better than life, my lips

will praise Thee. . . . When I remember Thee on my bed, I meditate on Thee in the night watches, for Thou hast been my help, for
Thou hast been my help, and in the shadow of Thy wings I sing
for joy. My soul *clings* to Thee; Thy right hand upholds me (emphasis added, NASB).

David got so spiritually dry that all he could do was tell God
and cling to Him. But in the clinging, he was faithful to worship,
pray, and meditate.

What do you do if you are so spiritually dry that you don't
want to worship, pray, and meditate? I think you should tell God
how you feel and do the best you can. You don't have to experience happy emotions in order to love and cling to God. You can
simply say, "As an act of love, manifested by my simple obedience, I offer you my prayer. I offer you my worship. I don't feel
that I am getting anything out of it, but it means something to me
to know that it is a way of demonstrating that I really do want to
love You."

So let us remember that we can cling to God by doing three
things. First, realize that the drought is not permanent. It will end.
Second, try to bring the circumstances of our lives under control,
so that we are not bringing spiritual dryness on ourselves unnec-
essarily. Third, do what we know we should do of the spiritual
disciplines even when we don't feel like it. It is an act of love to
God which He will reward.

How Do We Cling to God When We Don't Know What to Do?

We must cling to truth, counsel, and wisdom, believing that God is leading
us even when we discern no evidence of it.

A third time when we must cling to God is when we have lost
our way. When we don't know what to do. We don't know what
God's will is, and yet we have to do something. Or at least we
have to decide not to do something.

How many times have you had to make a decision, perfectly
willing to do God's will, but without any real confidence that you
knew what God's will was? If you are like a lot of us, you have
done it many times. But often the situation is more difficult than
just a quick decision. You would like to change jobs, but it would

require a move out of state, and such a move would be hard on your family. What do you do? Or, you would like to get married, but have not met anyone you feel comfortable marrying. You can't imagine that God wants you single the rest of your life, but neither can you imagine marrying anyone you currently know. You might do some things to try to meet others, and yet you feel a little funny about that. What do you do?

You are trying to decide what school to go to, or what job to take, or who to marry, or where to live, or a hundred other big things, and you want to do God's will, but simply cannot figure out what it is. This is a time to cling to God. At times you will know the will of God only when you look backwards. At times you simply will not know what to do, and yet you will be forced to make a decision anyway. Cling to God. Trust Him. Count on Him to be faithful to you and to His word, to lead you even though you don't feel led.

Conclusion

In the book *Adrift*, Steve Callahan tells the story of sailing the Atlantic Ocean, not far off the coast of Spain, when his sailboat was destroyed. At the last instant, he was able to salvage his life raft and a few emergency items. Amazingly, he drifted until he landed on a Caribbean island. It is a compelling story of endurance and determination.

As I read the book, I was struck with the relationship Callahan had with his life raft. When the seas were calm, he took little notice of his raft. He would even jump out of it and swim around, taking the raft for granted. But when the winds picked up, he would think seriously about his life raft. He would wonder if it would hold him. He would contemplate his raft, investigate it, even feel gratitude for it. But when the sudden and violent storms that stalk the Atlantic in the summer would swoop down on him like a hawk on a hapless chicken, that is when his relationship with the raft was the purest. He didn't jump out of the raft and swim around, nor sit and contemplate it. Rather, he wedged himself deep down inside his raft, buried himself in it, and clung to it until the storm is over.

When we feel adrift in the sea of life, when we feel at the mercy of circumstances around us, God is still our raft. In the easy times, we may take our raft for granted. We might even jump out of it and swim around lazily, gazing at our raft from a distance. But when the winds pick up we find ourselves wanting to get in our raft. We think about God. We investigate Him, we analyze Him, we ponder him. But it is during the storms of life that our relationship with God may be at its purest. We bury ourselves in the deepest recesses of God that we know, and we simply hang on until the storm is over.

We also have an advantage with God that Steve Callahan didn't have with his raft. God has promised to never leave us or forsake us (Hebrews 13:5). Are you hurting? Do you cope with physical pain, or are you burdened with emotional pain? Are you going through a spiritually dry time? Do you feel adrift, uncertain, confused? Do you feel at the mercy of circumstances? Cling to God. Listen to His promises:

> Trust in the Lord with all your heart, and do not lean on your own understanding. In all your ways acknowledge him, and he shall direct your paths (Proverbs 3:5–6 NASB).
>
> Cast your burden on the Lord, and he will sustain you (Psalm 55:22 NASB).
>
> He will cover you with his feathers, and under His wings you may seek refuge; His faithfulness is a shield and a bulwark. You will not be afraid of the terror by night, or of the arrow that flies by day; of the pestilence that stalks in darkness, or of the destruction that lays waste at noon. A thousand may fall at your side, and ten thousand at your right hand, but it shall not approach you (Psalm 91:4–7 NASB).
>
> The Lord liveth, and blessed be my rock and let the God of my salvation be exalted (Psalm 18:46 NASB).

Take God at His word. Say to yourself that no matter what comes I will cling to God: I will cling to my conviction that He will somehow see me through, even though there are times when it looks impossible. Mother Teresa once said something like, "When we get to heaven, our suffering on earth will be little more in comparison than a bad night in a cheap hotel."

Speed Bump!

Slow down to be sure you've gotten the main points of this chapter.

Question
Answer

Q1. How do we cling to God when it hurts?

A1. When we are in pain, we must trust the Scriptures and use the pain to force us *closer* to God rather than drive us farther from Him.

Q2. How do we cling to God when we are spiritually dry?

A2. We must believe that the drought will eventually end and continue to be *faithful* to the spiritual disciplines.

Q3. How do we cling to God when we don't know what to do?

A3. We must cling to truth, counsel, and wisdom, believing that God is leading us even when we discern no *evidence* of it.

Fill In the Blank

Question
Answer

Q1. How do we cling to God when it hurts?

A1. When we are in pain, we must trust the Scriptures and use the pain to force us _____ to God rather than drive us farther from Him.

Q2. How do we cling to God when we are spiritually dry?

A2. We must believe that the drought will eventually end and continue to be _____ to the spiritual disciplines.

Q3. How do we cling to God when we don't know what to do?

A3. We must cling to truth, counsel, and wisdom, believing that God is leading us even when we discern no _____ of it.

For Discussion and Thought

1. When was the last time things were going so badly for you that all you could do was cling to God? Perhaps it is now.

2. Are you hurting most in physical pain, spiritual drought, or spiritual indecision?

3. What insights have you gained from this material that have helped you the most?

4. Which area are you failing the most in? Spiritual disciplines? Trusting God during a dry time? Enduring pain? What could you do that would be most helpful for you?

5. Do you know others who are hurting badly but are not clinging to God? What could you tell them that would help them?

What If I Don't Believe?

1. If I don't believe this information about clinging to God, I will be left to my own human resources to see me through the difficulty.

2. I will have little sense of the presence of God and may even feel abandoned by Him because He does not relieve the suffering.

3. I may wonder what I have done to deserve what I'm are going through, as though God were punishing me for something, when in actuality He is not.

For Further Study

1. Scripture.
There are passages in the Bible that speak about clinging to God. They include:

- Psalm 22:1–3

- Isaiah 40:27–41

- Lamentations 3:1–28

2. Books.
There are other helpful books for studying this subject further. They are listed below in general order of difficulty. If I could only read one of these, I would read the first one:

You Gotta Keep Dancing, Tim Hansel
Where Is God When It Hurts? Philip Yancey
Disappointment With God, Philip Yancey
A Grief Observed, C.S. Lewis
The Problem of Pain, C.S. Lewis

> *A man can no more diminish God's glory by refusing to worship Him than a lunatic can put out the sun by scribbling the word "darkness" on the walls of his cell.*
> ■ **C. S. Lewis**

12

How Do We Worship God?

As we head into the twenty-first century, we find that we are a people starved for relationships. Ironically, we are not starved for contact with people; we are starved for satisfying relationships. We may enter a friendship and unfortunately come *out* of it still hungry for relationship. We may enter a marriage and, sadly, still long for relationship. We may go to church and also come away hungry for relationships. We may even go to God and, unbelievably, still be hungry for relationship.

Why is it that hunger is characteristic of our day? There is no one simple answer, but I am persuaded that it is a result of the kind of nation we have become. We live in a fast-paced culture dominated by technology. Priorities on God and people have been replaced by values on money, success, possessions, technology, progress, and *self*. As a result, we have gotten what we value: money, success, possessions, technology, progress, and *self*. And we have lost what we did not value: God and people. We have lost significant relationships.

We no longer appreciate the importance of relationships, and we seem to have lost the willingness to develop them. The same is true of our relationship with God. We are no longer inclined to pay the price for having a significant relationship with Him, because we have so many other "priorities." And our relationship with God is only as rich as our worship of Him. However, we are in a crisis of worship. An acute hunger for worship grows within Christians all around the world. I have linked "worship" with the general problem of "relationships" because I want us to see that we face an overall challenge. Our trouble finding significance and meaning in worshipping God is not isolated. It is part of a general problem. Therefore, it should not surprise us that the solution is not an isolated solution, but a more general one.

I referred in a previous chapter to a comment from Carl Sandburg, who said, "Without great audiences, there can be no great poets." It takes a great audience to recognize the greatness of God. Today, however, our culture is fast losing its capacity to recognize even human greatness, let alone God's greatness. If we are losing our ability to ap-

---

In this chapter we learn . . .

1. True worship is the complete offering of our complete selves to God.
2. We worship God personally by making a total life commitment to Him.
3. We worship God corporately by coming to Him in a spirit of true worship, and then engaging in activities designed to publicly give God the worth due Him.
4. We can become better worshippers by making worship a higher priority.

---

preciate greatness, it is no surprise that we are losing our ability to produce it. With rare exceptions, we produce no great poetry, no great music, no great literature, no great ideas. To compound this problem, we pay athletes and movie stars millions of dollars to entertain us, but artists, writers, and thinkers cannot make a living. I am saying that a culture tends to get what it values; and today, we value entertainment more than other forms of greatness. Consequently, we are rapidly losing our ability to appreciate it or even to recognize it.

This influence hinders even earnest Christians from fully worshipping God. But this is not God's problem. It is the audience's problem. One of our tasks, then is to become a greater audience. And it can be done. And when we do, when the greatness of God fills our minds like the oceans fill the depths of the earth, we will be fully worshipping God.

What Is True Worship?

True worship is the complete offering of our complete selves to God.

Several Hebrew and Greek words in the Bible are translated "worship." But there is only one main Hebrew word for "worship" in the Old Testament and one main Greek word for "worship" in the New Testament. Both mean the same thing. Yet it does not mean "to sing," or "to gather together in a congregation," or "to go through a ceremony," or even "to get quiet and solemn." The word "to worship" literally means "to prostrate oneself, to fall down on one's face."

I admit that I was surprised by that. I don't think the word must always be taken literally. It can also mean, in a figurative sense, to spiritually prostrate oneself before God.

Does that puzzle you, as it did me? What is intended by a word that means "to prostrate oneself"? When we prostrate ourselves figuratively before God, what are we doing? If we don't understand that we may not know what it means to worship.

Let's imagine what would be going on in our hearts and minds if we prostrated ourselves before someone else. If I prostrated myself before someone, I would be recognizing his authority. I would be affirming his superiority. I would be demonstrating my submission. I would be placing myself at his mercy and disposal. It would be a massive gesture of total personal offering and sacrifice. In the land of the free and the home of the brave, in the land where all men are equal, in the land of rugged individualism, we can hardly imagine prostrating ourselves like that. But if we did, we would be saying by our body language that "You are greater than we are, and we recognize that. We humble ourselves before You, place ourselves at your mercy and disposal, and agree to do anything You tell us to do." Here is an act of total sacrifice.

True worship equals a total commitment.

So, when the Bible uses the word "worship" it means more than we may have thought. In John 4:23–24, we read, "an hour is coming, and now is, when the true worshipers shall worship the Father in spirit and truth; for such people the father seeks to be His worshipers. God is spirit; and those who worship Him must worship in spirit and truth" (NASB). To paraphrase, God seeks people who will give themselves to Him totally. He is seeking people who will say, "You are greater than I am, and I recognize that. I humble myself to you, I place myself at your mercy and disposal, and I agree to do anything you tell me to do."

Is that what you do on Sunday mornings? Worship, in its fundamental meaning, is an offering of the complete self to God. Unless we understand that, we will misunderstand both what *we* do in worship and what *God* requires. As a result, we will miss the deep and meaningful relationship with God that we long to have.

How Do We Worship God Personally?

We worship God personally by making a total life commitment to Him.

Do you have a regular, satisfying time of worshiping the Lord alone? You are in a minority if you do. Many people find it almost impossible to develop any regularity at daily devotions with the Lord.

Why is that? One reason is that we have trouble disciplining ourselves to do anything regularly. We have trouble exercising, we have trouble dieting, we have trouble keeping our car clean and well maintained. A second reason is that we are so busy. A third reason is that we don't get anything out of our time with God. We are faithful spending time with God on a daily basis for a few days or week or few weeks, but eventually, rigor mortis sets in, we stiffen up, and our quiet times are gone.

The reason? One reason is that nothing always excites us. Our first Fourth of July fireworks show probably mesmerized us. Now, we take it in stride.

Another reason, as has been mentioned, is that we are not yet a great audience. Our minds have become so secularized and so trivialized that our tastes no longer enjoy great things. How, then, do we develop a taste for great things? In the chapter on pursuing God, we recognized that we can change what our taste buds enjoy. But only after a time of tastelessness, during which we must simply "tough" things out. We can lessen our taste for sugar and heighten our taste for healthy foods by cutting down on sugar and eating more healthy foods, but the healthier foods will not be as enjoyable to us at first.

The same thing is true mentally, emotionally, and spiritually. On a personal level, we must cut out our spiritual sugar, and begin consuming more spiritually healthy things so that we can develop a taste for great things. When we develop a taste for greater things, we have a greater appreciation for God and His Word.

Disciplining ourselves for personal worship is difficult, but rewarding.

Practically speaking, the same mind that will laugh at smutty television sitcoms will not marvel at God. The mind that savors sensual rock videos will not fully appreciate God. The two things are so opposed that no one mind can well embrace both. You must understand that you are making a choice when you fill your mind with the trivial, the sensual, and the violent. You are alienating yourself from God. So, if you want to begin appreciating God, you must eliminate mental and spiritual junk and poison from your diet.

Whenever I make these kinds of comments, I always get a few charges of "legalism." It is no more legalism to state these dangers clearly than it is to warn of the physical dangers of too much sugar, or too much cholesterol, or too much caffeine. If it is indeed a danger, it is not legalism to warn of the danger.

So when you sit down to try to get something out of your time with God, it is not as simple as just carving out the time. What you will get out of a one-half hour session with God will depend largely on what you are doing with yourself the other $23\frac{1}{2}$ hours of the day. If you are not getting enough rest, you will get little out of your time with God. If you are filling your mind with trivial or immoral things, you will get little out of your time with God. It is just like, if you are drinking a lot of alcohol, smoking cigarettes, eating high cholesterol food, not getting enough sleep, and under a lot of stress, then taking a One-A-Day multi-vitamin is going to do very little good. You need an overall change.

Worshipping God on a personal level is not a matter of spending a few minutes with Him, and a Bible, and a daily devotional book. It is a matter of total life commitment. It is a matter of prostrating yourself before Him, spiritually, and all that that means, 24 hours a day. Worshipping God cannot be compartmentalized.

How Do We Worship God Corporately?

We worship God corporately by coming to Him in a spirit of true worship, and then engaging in activities designed to publicly give God the worth due Him.

Finding a church to worship that you are happy with is a big deal. My wife Margie and I have lived several places where it seemed we just could not find a church that we were really happy with. It left an enormous hole in our lives. Something terribly important was missing. Many of you know what I mean. There is no one church that can satisfy all Christians, just as there is no one restaurant that can satisfy all patrons. Our tastes differ, so one church will be best for one person, and another church will be best for another person. In addition, one church may meet our needs for a number of years, but as we grow older, our perspective and values might change, and so we may feel a need to find another church. That is perfectly understandable and perfectly acceptable.

The only thing I would add to that is that once you have found the church that is best for you, you must make that church your home, and accept it, weaknesses and all. You become a part of it and try to help make it a better place, from the inside out. It is your church, and the people are your people, and you are committed and loyal to it while it is your church. If it should come to the point at which you cannot give your church your loyalty, it is time to ask God either to correct the problem, or to give you another church.

Many of us believe (I confess that for a long time I held this idea) that when you come to a worship service you are coming to an event which other people put on for you. You are a spectator and other people are the performers—the musicians and the preacher particularly. Worship, then, becomes entertainment, and the goal is often to be moved emotionally. I now understand that that is incorrect. In true worship, God is the audience, the congregation acts, and the worship team, including the minister, helps the congregation to participate. Worship, therefore, is active, not passive. It matters whether or not we participate.

Why Do I Need to Know This?

1. If I don't understand that worship is a total commitment of my life, I may believe that worship is only a religious activity.
2. I might not understand that religious activity is important only if it is founded on a total commitment of one's life to God.
3. I might believe that worship activities are passive "shows" which I attend, rather than opportunities for me to participate in from the heart.
4. I might not understand that to fail in the pursuit of meaningful worship is to miss out on a fundamental responsibility and opportunity for God's blessing.

Also, if worship is a matter of prostrating one's self before God, it is not necessary to be moved emotionally every time. It is more important that the mind be engaged than that the heart be moved. Now if the mind is truly engaged, that will encourage the heart to be moved. But, on the other hand, you can be moved emotionally without having your mind engaged.

That is one of the dangers of emotionally charged services. Today's popular short choruses, for example, and many of which

I *like,* are enjoyable little songs. And they are easy to hum throughout the week. But many of them have very simple

Corporate worship focuses our acts on the audience—God.

messages, such as the chorus "Alleluia," which is a single word sung slowly over and over again. The intellectual teeth of that word is not what is attractive. It is the emotion evoked by the music. The melody, the chord progressions, and the repetition get us emotionally involved. No problem as far as that goes. But if all that is sung is content-weak, emotionally evocative songs, it shrinks worship to mere emotional involvement.

Again, worship is the spiritual prostrating of ourselves before God. In corporate worship this would include the acceptance and affirmation of biblical truths, perhaps through public readings, songs, and prayers. It is declaring to God the wonder of who He is and what He has done. You cannot do that through simple choruses alone.

On the other hand, many people are not moved by traditional hymns and "higher" music. That is why I believe that balancing the two can bring a greater strength than only one or the other. You can sing some choruses and then some traditional hymns. In special music, sometimes it can be more contemporary and sometimes more traditional. This creates a good balance, a more complete act of worship, than if we insisted on one or the other. The make-up of the congregation will also influence how much of one and how much of the other is required for balance in that congregation.

Nor is corporate worship all singing. Nor is it all preaching. If all we did were to sing a hymn, pass the plate, and listen to fifty minutes of preaching, we might be having a grand Bible study, but many of us would not be worshipping. Bible teaching tends to leave the audience passive, and worship must be active. Balance—that is the key. We must balance the activity of singing, prayer, and affirming creeds and statements of faith with listening to special music and preaching.

When we understand what true worship is, we recognize God's authority, affirm His superiority, demonstrate our submission, and place ourselves at His mercy and disposal. In corporate worship the entire congregation ought to have this attitude. If so, they will engage in activities designed to give God the public praise and recognition that are rightfully His.

How Can We Become Better Worshippers?

We can become better worshippers by making worship a higher priority.

In her excellent little book *Up With Worship*, Anne Ortlund writes:

> When I was little we used to play church. We'd get the chairs into rows, fight over who'd be preacher, vigorously lead the hymn singing, and generally have a great carnal time.
>
> The aggressive kids naturally wanted to be up front, directing or preaching. The quieter ones were content to sit and be entertained by the up-fronters.
>
> Occasionally we'd get mesmerized by a true sensationalistic crowd-swayer—like the girl who said, "Boo, I'm the Holy Ghost!" But in general, if the up-fronters were pretty good they could hold their audience quite a while. If they weren't so good, eventually the kids would drift off to play something else—like jump rope or jacks.
>
> Now that generation has grown up, but most of them haven't changed too much. Every Sunday they still play church. They line up in rows for the entertainment. If it's pretty good, their church may grow. If it's not too hot, eventually they'll drift off to play something else.

Ah, worship. What is it, and how do we do it? It is easy to get confused and substitute other things for worship. Many years ago Thomas K. Beecher once preached for his brother, Henry Ward Beecher, at the Plymouth Church in Brooklyn, New York. Henry was a famous preacher, and many people had come to hear him. When Thomas stood up to preach, some people began to move toward the doors. Realizing that they were disappointed because he was substituting for his brother, Thomas raised his hand for silence and announced, "All those who came here this morning to worship Henry Ward Beecher may leave now. All who came to worship the Lord may remain."

It happens to us, doesn't it? We go to church not because God is there but because a certain preacher is there, or a certain choir or vocalist. There is nothing wrong with enjoying good preaching and music, but those are only aids to worship. *God* is why we worship. We have to be sure we are getting it right.

We can be great worshippers. We can begin to grasp the great themes, and take greater pleasure in God than ever before. You can enjoy God. You can enjoy your time with Him. You can find the good things in your heart, and then tell God that you really mean them.

I think there are four steps to begin cultivating a capacity for great worship:

1. *Decide to care about worshipping Him.* Many of the things we value in life we decided to value. We must value worship of God. We must sit back and ask ourselves: what is important to me? What do I want to live for the rest of my life? And then, we must decide to include worshiping God. Decide to become a great audience.

2. *Fill your life with great people.* The easiest way to become different is to hang around people who are like how we want to become. So hang around them. Ask them over for dinner. Go to a concert with them. Ask them over to your house for conversation. Take them boating on the lake or something else . . . anything else, but get time with them. And then, talk about spiritual things. Go below the surface. Transcend news, weather, and sports. One of Margie's and my favorites is to ask people how they became Christians. Or something else might work for you. But fill your lives with great people.

3. *Fill your lives with great pursuits.* Find something noble to do, and do it. One thing, if one is all you have time for. It might be helping cancer patients. It might be visiting prisoners. It might be teaching children's Sunday school. It might be teaching adults how to read, or fighting abortion or becoming a really good usher or holding seminars at work which will help people, or something else, but fill your lives with great pursuits. Of course, the only way you will have time is to drop off the trivial things that keep you from great pursuits.

4. *Fill your minds with great thoughts.* Read things that build you up. Talk with people who challenge you. Watch selectively movies or television that encourages you to be a better, bigger person. Think. Carve out time for solitude and quiet, so that your mind can find its true equilibrium. I don't think a person can live a balanced Christian life unless he has adequate amounts of time alone where it is quiet. Write. Keep a journal. Correspond with edifying friends. Fill your minds with great things.

As you do these four things—decide to become a greater audience, fill your life with great people, fill your lives with great pursuits, and fill your life with great thoughts—you will become a greater audience, and worshiping God will become a more meaningful part of your life. Of course, like all things, some days are better than others, and not every day will be better than the last. That is a trap we can get into that is pretty hard on us. We feel we fail if today is not as good or better than yesterday. But when we remind ourselves that worship is does not depend on emotions, we can experiment with things that work for us, changing our procedure often, if that is helpful, and then we can develop a satisfying life of personal and corporate worship.

Every Sunday morning, something goes on that is a highlight in my life. I worship together with other like-minded Christians. Take away my speaking engagements, my travel, the books I've written . . . take them all away. But don't take away my Sunday morning worship, and don't take away my every-morning and every-evening time with God. If you don't feel this way already, you can. Be patient. It will take time. But meaningful personal and corporate worship can be yours.

Speed Bump!
Slow dow to be sure you've gotten the main points of this chapter.

Question Answer

Q1. What is true worship?

A1. True worship is the complete offering of our complete *selves* to God.

Q2. How do we worship God personally?

A2. We worship God personally by making a total life *commitment* to Him.

Q3. How do we worship God corporately?

A3. We worship God corporately by coming to Him in a spirit of true worship, and then engaging in activities designed to publicly give God the *worth* due Him.

Q4. How can we become better worshipers?

A4. We can become better worshippers by making worship a higher *priority*.

Fill In the Blank

Question   **Q1.** What is true worship?

Answer   **A1.** True worship is the complete offering of our complete _____ to God.

Q2. How do we worship God personally?

A2. We worship God personally by making a total life _____ to Him.

Q3. How do we worship God corporately?

A3. We worship God corporately by coming to Him in a spirit of true worship, and then engaging in activities designed to publicly give God the _____ due Him.

Q4. How can we become better worshipers?

A4. We can become better worshippers by making worship a higher _____.

For Discussion and Thought

1. Are you satisfied with your personal worship? If not, what is the problem? Do you merely need some fine tuning or good ideas about daily tools and strategies to use, or does your whole life need reorientation?

2. Are you satisfied with corporate worship? If not, how do you need to reevaluate your role in corporate worship from a spectator to a participant?

3. What can you do as an individual to help improve the corporate worship of your church?

4. What is your opinion as to what an ideal worship service should be like? Has your opinion changed due to reading this chapter?

What If I Don't Believe?

If I don't believe in these principles of personal and corporate worship:

1. I am not likely to view worship activities as part of an overall life which must reflect total commitment to God in everything I do.

2. I am not likely to exercise the discipline or creativity necessary to have a satisfying experience of personal worship.

3. I am not likely to get involved enough to qualify as a participant and not just a spectator in corporate worship.

For Further Study

1. Scripture.
Several passages will enhance our study of worship.

- 1 Chronicles 16:28–29

- John 4:20–24

- Romans 12:1–2

- 1 Corinthians 14:25

- Revelation 4 & 5

Read these passages and consider how they integrate with the material discussed in this chapter.

2. Books.
There are several helpful books for studying this subject further. They are listed below in general order of difficulty. If I could read only one of these, I would read the first one:

Up With Worship, Anne Ortlund
Real Worship, Warren Wiersbe
Worship, the Ultimate Priority, John MacArthur

Bibliography

Barclay, William. *The Letters to Galatians and Ephesians*. Philadelphia: The Westminster Press, 1958.

Davies, P.C.W. "The Tailor-made Universe," *The Sciences*. May-June, 1978, 6–10.

Hoyle, Sir Fred. "The Big Bang in Astronomy," *The New Scientist*. Nov., 1981.

Jastro, Robert. "God's Creation," *Science Digest*. Special Spring Issue, 1980.

Lewis, C.S. *A Grief Observed*. New York: The Seabury Press, 1961.

_____. *The Weight of Glory and Other Addresses*. Grand Rapids: Eerdmans, 1965.

MacDonald, Gordon. *Ordering Your Private World*. Nashville: Oliver-Nelson, 1985.

McGrath, Alister. *Understanding the Trinity*. Grand Rapids: Zondervan, 1988.

Morely, Patrick. *The Man in the Mirror*. Nashville: Thomas Nelson Publishers, 1989.

Ortlund, Anne. *Up With Worship*. Ventura, CA: Regal Books, 1975.

Ostling, Richard. "Kingdoms to Come," *Time*. Special Issue, Fall, 1992.

Packer, James I. *Concise Theology*. Wheaton, IL: Tyndale, 1993.

Pascal, Blaise. *Pascal's Pensées*. W. F. Trotter, trans. New York: E. P. Dutton, 1958.

Sullivan, Deidre. *What Do We Mean When We Say God?* New York: Doubleday, 1990.

ten Boom, Corrie. *The Hiding Place*. Uhrichsville, OH: Barbour and Company, 1971.

Weaver, Kenneth. "The Incredible Universe," *National Geographic*. May, 1974.

Willard, Dallas. *The Spirit of the Disciplines*. San Francisco: Harper & Row, 1988.

Yancey, Philip. *Disappointment With God*. Grand Rapids: Zondervan, 1988.

Master Review

Chapter 1

Question
Answer

Q1. How does God explain the existence in the universe?

A1. Every effect must have an adequate cause, and God is the only cause adequate for the existence of the universe.

Q2. How does God explain the order and purpose in the universe?

A2. The order and purpose in the universe suggest an intelligent creator behind it.

Q3. How does God explain the uniqueness of humanity?

A3. Humankind is a higher being than all other animals, and being created in the image of God explains why.

Q4. How does biblical evidence demand the existence of God?

A4. The Bible concurs with our observations about life and the universe, and describes the God who made it.

Chapter 2

Q1. How do we define "God"?

A1. God is an infinite, eternal spirit, creator of the universe and sovereign over it.

Q2. What characteristics does God share with humanity?

A2. Among the characteristics which God shares with humanity are His moral characteristics of holiness, love, justice, and goodness.

Chapter 3

Q1. Does God have a beginning and an end?

A1. God is eternal, existing without a beginning or an end.

Q2. Does God ever change?

A2. God is immutable; He has never changed and will never change.

Q3. Is God everywhere?

A3. God is omnipresent; He is everywhere simultaneously.

Q4. Does God know everything?

A4. God is omniscient; He knows all things, both actual and possible.

Q5. Can God do anything He wants?

A5. God is omnipotent; He can do whatever He chooses.

Chapter 4

Q1. How many Gods does the Bible teach there are?

A1. The Bible teaches that there is only one God.

Q2. Who are Jesus and the Holy Spirit?

A2. In addition to God the Father, Jesus and the Holy Spirit are also called God in the Bible.

Q3. Can the doctrine of the Trinity be fully explained?

A3. Attempts to explain the doctrine of the Trinity fully fall short, as do all attempts to explain God fully. The statements of Scripture that form this doctrine must be taken by faith at face value.

Chapter 5

Q1. Who is God the Father?

A1. The Father is God, the first member of the Trinity.

Q2. What does God the Father do?

A2. God the Father initiates in His relationship within the Trinity, and He provides for and protects His children.

Q3. How do we worship God the Father?

A3. We worship God the Father in the sincerity of our heart, ascribing with words and deeds the worth due Him.

Chapter 6

Q1. What hope does God give us?

A1. God gives us hope in the challenges of life in this world and hope for eternal life in the next.

Q2. What moral values does God give us?

A2. God gives us a secure basis for truth and falsehood, and for good and evil.

Q3. What does God give us to live for?

A3. God satisfies the deepest longings of our souls.

Chapter 7

Q1. How can we learn about God?

A1. We learn about God through the Bible, through nature, and through our conscience.

Q2. How do we meet God?

A2. We meet God by saying "yes" to God's invitation to come to Him.

Q3. How can we grow in our relationship with God?

A3. We grow in our relationship with God when we learn of God's character and commands, and then trust and obey Him.

Chapter 8

Q1. What is our greatest natural desire?

A1. Our greatest natural desire is to be happy.

Q2. What are the most dangerous counterfeits?

A2. The most dangerous counterfeits of happiness are money, beauty, and talent.

Q3. What is the source of true happiness?

A3. God alone is the source of true happiness.

Q4. What must we guard in our pursuit of God?

A4. In our pursuit of God, we must guard our spiritual disciplines, our environment, and our choice of friends.

Chapter 9

Q1. How must we treat God's commandments?

A1. We must obey His commandments to demonstrate our love for God.

Q2. How must we treat our resources?

A2. God has given each of us the three basic resources of time, talent, and treasures, and we must commit those resources to Him.

Q3. How must we treat others?

A3. How we love others is a test of how we love God.

Chapter 10

Q1. What is the most difficult question people ask?

A1. The most difficult question people ask is, "Why does God not relieve human suffering?"

Q2. How do we reconcile our pain with God's character?

A2. We recognize that there are spiritual realities that transcend our comprehension.

Q3. How is Jesus our example in suffering?

A3. Jesus set the example of total trust and obedience to God, even in suffering.

Chapter 11

Q1. How do we cling to God when it hurts?

A1. When we are in pain, we must trust the Scriptures and use the pain to force us closer to God rather than drive us farther from Him.

Q2. How do we cling to God when we are spiritually dry?

A2. We must believe that the drought will eventually end and continue to be faithful to the spiritual disciplines.

Q3. How do we cling to God when we don't know what to do?

A3. We must cling to truth, counsel, and wisdom, believing that God is leading us even when we discern no evidence of it.

Chapter 12

Q1. What is true worship?

A1. True worship is the complete offering of our complete selves to God.

Q2. How do we worship God personally?

A2. We worship God personally by making a total life commitment to Him.

Q3. How do we worship God corporately?

A3. We worship God corporately by coming to Him in a spirit of true worship, and then engaging in activities designed to publicly give God the worth due Him.

Q4. How can we become better worshipers?

A4. We can become better worshipers by making worship a higher priority.

About the Author

Max Anders is a pastor at heart who applies the truths of God's word to people's everyday lives. An original team member with Walk Thru the Bible Ministries and pastor of a mega-church for a number of years before beginning his speaking and writing ministry, Max has traveled extensively, speaking to thousands across the country.

His books include *30 Days to Understanding the Bible, 30 Days to Understanding the Christian Life, 30 Days to Understanding What Christians Believe,* and (as co-author) *Drawing Near.* He holds a Master of Theology degree from Dallas Theological Seminary and a doctorate from Western Seminary in Portland, Oregon.

If you are interested in having Max Anders speak at your conference, church, or special event, please call interAct Speaker's Bureau at 1-800-370-9932.